Mom
and Me in the
Kitchen

Mom and Me in the Kitchen

Memories of Our Mothers' Kitchens

A
Fix-It and Forget-It
FAMILY BOOK

by **Phyllis Pellman Good**
and the friends of the *Fix-It and Forget-It* series

Good Books

Intercourse, PA 17534
800/762-7171
www.GoodBooks.com

Design by Cliff Snyder

MOM AND ME IN THE KITCHEN
Copyright © 2013 by Good Books, Intercourse, PA 17534
International Standard Book Number: 978-1-56148-793-6
Library of Congress Control Number: 2013932403

Publisher's Cataloging-in-Publication Data
Good, Phyllis Pellman
    Mom and me in the kitchen : memories of our mothers' kitchens
/ Phyllis Pellman Good and the friends of the Fix-It and Forget-It
series.
    p. cm.
    ISBN 978-1-56148-793-6
    "A Fix-it and Forget-It Family Book."

1. Cooking, American. 2. Mothers --Anecdotes. 3. Mother and child
--Anecdotes. I. Title.

TX715 .G6366 2013
641.5973 --dc23   2013932403

Contents

Meet My Mom –
and Lots of Other Moms!

Think about the home you grew up in. What part did the kitchen play? Was your mom usually there? Did you show up just to eat, or was the kitchen a gathering place for other activities?

I love stories. I love how telling stories is contagious. You tell a story, which reminds me of a story—and then we're off—trading memories, talking over each other, remembering things we hadn't thought about for years.

We asked our *Fix-It and Forget-It* friends for stories about their moms, especially their moms' part in making meals and caring for them, often in the kitchen.

I asked them these six questions to jog their memories:

1. **Tell us about your mom when you were growing up.**

- How'd she look?

- What did she like to do?

- What was important to her?

- What food did she like to make?

- What did you and she do together?

2. What was mealtime like at your home when you were growing up?

- Who cooked?

- What foods do you remember?

- Did you all sit down and eat together?

- Was the TV on?

- How were picky eaters dealt with?

- What do you remember talking about?

3. Tell about a kitchen accident—or an embarrassing incident—that you remember.

- What happened?

- Who was involved?

- Was your mom home?

- What was the outcome?

4. Tell about a birthday meal—or another special meal— that your mom made for you one time.

- What did you have to eat?

- What made it a special time?

5. How did you learn to cook?

- Who helped you?

- What did s/he do to help you learn?

- What did you make?

- How old were you?

6. **If you could go back to one time in the kitchen with your mom while you were growing up, when would it be?**

- What happened?

- What makes that time stand out to you?

Then I answered those questions with my own mom stories. I dug out old photos. And I started telling my kids what I remembered. Then they started in with their memories of me and our kitchen! See what I mean.

I hope you enjoy this collection of little treasures. I hope they stir up memories and stories you have of your mom— and maybe of being a mom.

This is some of what makes us who we are, folks!

Phyllis Pellman Good

Mom Herself

My mom was young, energetic, and always busy. She spent hours every summer in her continuously-expanding garden, which makes sense in retrospect since she grew up on a farm. When I was young, that was part of what always made me associate her with the colors blue (the sky) and green (her plants).

She was always focused on bringing healthy foods into our lives, though some methods were more successful than others. The tofu she hid in a stir-fry was identified by my dad as "toad food" and therefore never eaten again.

Her use of the vegetable garden was truly inspired. We were allowed to plant our own carrots in the very front row, and despite my aversion to other carrots served at meals, I would always eat the ones I grew all by myself.

While fresh foods were an easy one with my mom, she was not the main cook in the household. Most dinners were headed up by my dad since my mom was often out driving us to our practices for sports. She was incredibly supportive of our competitions and shows and did not miss a day until my sister and I were both old enough to drive.

The limited cooking may have made the things she did make more special. I will never forget how she made home-made chicken noodle soup whenever we were sick, Dutch apple pies every Thanksgiving for our family and friends, sugar cookies every Christmas, and the most amazing baking powder biscuits on cold winter nights.

My mom always made a special treat for us to take to school on our birthdays.

One of my earliest memories is sitting on the counter, kicking my legs, and singing, "Mama's little baby loves shortenin', shortenin', Mama's little baby loves shortenin' bread," while she made shortbread. To this day, I can't make it without smiling and singing that to myself. I hope some day my baby girl has a similar memory that brings her as much joy about her time with me. ❧ *Angela Hallisy*

❧

My mother was a kind, caring, giving person. She always put others first before herself, especially her husband who didn't respect her as he should have.

My mother cooked German food, which was my father's influence. We often had sauerkraut and dumplings; I have yet to be able to duplicate her dumplings as mine either turn out too sticky or burnt.

My mother's giving nature and kindness has made me the same as her. My husband loves me for my gentle nature and my generosity to others. ❧ *Natalie Mueller*

My mom always had a look of strength about her. She learned survival at a very young age, growing up during the Great Depression. Her mother died when she was 12, but Mom had already learned to sew from scraps, iron for a few coins, and rent toys. Her mother was poor, so Mom spent the remainder of her childhood at a work farm/orphanage. That's why the most important thing in her life was family.

Most of Mom's dishes were three steps from pantry to oven. They consisted of goulash, tuna casseroles, homemade mac and cheese, sauerkraut and pork, ham-beans, or good old-fashioned scalloped potatoes. I laugh about this now, but when I was a child, egg in a hole was the most awesome trick I had ever seen! It was not the size of the meal but the simplicity of it that warmed my heart.

Mom's menu was not fancy, but it was always seasoned with love. The green bowls were always filled with a bread pudding or a rice pudding with raisins. My greatest memory was the rolled sugar cookie recipe with 10x sugar, which we

Egg in a Hole
Lorraine Perry

1 Tbsp. butter
1 egg
1 slice of bread
salt/pepper to taste

1. Melt butter in skillet. Make a hole in the bread and lay it in the pan. Crack the egg into the hole.
2. Cook on low. When egg is firm, flip, and continue cooking until as brown as you like it.

still make to this day. Mom is 84 but looks forward to the tradition of me delivering those rolled cookies.

Mom grew up poor and stood in soup lines waiting for meals during the Depression, but she is rich with a mother's love. 　　　　　　　　　　　　　　　　　　🌶 *Lorraine Perry*

🌿

My mom didn't like to cook. Either that or her oven hated her. They were evenly matched.

🌶 *Lori Fleming Browne*

🌿

My mom was beautiful with sparkling blue eyes and a constant smile. She was a sharp cookie all her life and a great judge of character. She rarely left her kitchen. She was a true Southern lady who made one feel at home in her presence and surroundings. Both sides of my parents' families, and their families, neighbors, and friends filled her kitchen daily. For holidays, our home was the place to be. Everyone loved Aunt Ruth and her style of cooking.

She made simple Southern foods in a small, simple home. Always sweet tea and lemonade to drink. "Y'all come on in, sit down. I'll bring you a glass of sweet tea," was a common phrase. Another one was, "Are you hungry? There's plenty of so-and-so on the stove." She always had a huge pot of soup and cornbread or fried chicken or spaghetti or minute steaks or fried salmon patties or pork chops, country fried potatoes, stews, and Sunday roast.

Mom cooked basically the same recipes every week, repeated like a restaurant menu. We knew Friday night was spaghetti night, and so did everyone else. "Here they come,

Ruth," was heard every day at different times from my dad. They loved company and making people feel special and loved.

When she made fried chicken, she hid a breast for me in the cabinet since so many people might show up. We had cornbread and homemade biscuits at every meal, sometimes for breakfast with sorghum syrup and real homemade butter in a churn, which I have now.

I don't think there was a picky eater in the whole clan, but I refused to drink out of plastic. It smelled and had an off taste to me. I still prefer glass.   ❧ *Ann Scroggins Lucas*

❧

My mom was a very small woman, only 4' 10" tall. She was a public health nurse and worked with a wonderful doctor. She loved to collect dolls and all the things that went with them. She had a beautiful collection that she willed to the North Dakota Historical Society upon her passing.

Helping people in need was always important to her. She would always say, "There but for the grace of God go I." She would bring hobos into our kitchen and feed them a hearty meal, then pack a lunch for them to take with them. Sometimes she would give them clothes or a blanket to take when they left. Needless to say, she was very popular with the needy.

I loved the times she would take me downtown with her. She would get me a little cone of French fries and we would sit on a bench and eat them. This was especially thrilling at Christmas when we would go to see the decorations in the big department stores.

❧ *Helene M. Stafford*

When I was 9, we made strawberry jam. I got to hull the berries and crush them in the pan. She let me sit on a stool near her and watch the mixture bubble in the pan.

M om was a petite woman. Five feet tall, brunette, and full of energy. She had to be to raise five kids.

She made the most delicious homemade bread and buns. I remember watching her mixing the bread dough up in a huge aluminum pan. I have that pan now. I look at it, and I can almost smell that delicious bread baking.

When Mom made pudding for the family, she would let me stand on a stool beside her so I could watch, and sometimes she let me stir the pudding. She watched carefully over me so that I wouldn't get burned. She filled custard cups with the pudding, and she let me clean out the pudding pan. Mmmmmmm.

After we ate all the pudding, she would wash the custard cups, and since I always begged to help do dishes, she let me wash the spoons. I still have those custard cups fifty years later, and they carry wonderful memories of Mom.

When she was diagnosed with Alzheimer's, my heart stood still. She always feared it. Her mother and aunt had it too. It was very hard to see Mom going further and further away in her mind.   ✿ *Bonnie Pruett*

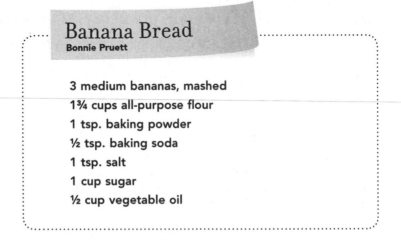

Banana Bread
Bonnie Pruett

3 medium bananas, mashed

1¾ cups all-purpose flour

1 tsp. baking powder

½ tsp. baking soda

1 tsp. salt

1 cup sugar

½ cup vegetable oil

2 large eggs
1 tsp. vanilla
¾ cup chopped walnuts or chocolate chips

1. Mix all ingredients thoroughly.
2. Pour into greased 9x5 loaf pan. Fill pan evenly.
3. Bake at 350° for 70-75 minutes or until a toothpick inserted in the center comes out clean. Let cool and pop the bread out of the pan.

M y mother is a petite woman with weathered hands. She has wonderfully shaped tough nails and that can describe my mother as a person. You could think that she is a quiet mousy person without an opinion. But she has a love for holidays, an off-beat sense of humor, and a high tolerance for blood and guts.

As a child, I would roam her laboratory with my siblings (Mom is a marine biologist). The older I got the more I helped out. One year I cleaned and fed two larval sea robins named Him and Her. I would weigh desiccated fish larvae for her experiments. I would occasionally draw pictures of her larval fish. And for a few years I electro-shocked fish as part of an experiment in a city river. When I got older, I entered data for her during her bay data collections. We would take my children to the zoo and share our love of animals and science.

My mother favors fresh vegetables, fresh meats, fresh fruits. She prefers frozen in the winter but will use canned as a last resort. Mom likes simple meals meaning few spices and few cooking steps. She uses herbs from her garden and whatever is ripe or in season. Red meat, fish, pork, white meat—Mom's not a vegetarian by far. She enjoys other cuisines in general as long as there are no legumes or hot spices in them.

My mother has kept a garden every year except the years she lived in Alaska and in Bristol. She has a green thumb and toils at raising four seasons' worth of food each year.

The family is very important to my mother. I don't know why. She's not a very nostalgic person and has a practical attitude towards events and other people. She's also usually so busy that it's hard to tell what she may be thinking. My mother has kept my secrets. To tell you that she is a saint wouldn't be right, and it would make her angry. She is one of the strongest, most stable people that I know. In a world full of chaos, my mother is a rock.   ✿ *A. MacPhee*

✿

My mother was tall and thin. She usually wore Shelton Stroller dresses or her nurse's uniform with starched hat, freshly polished white shoes, and seamed white stockings. She did not wear slacks for many years. She went to the hair dresser once a week. She had very few gray hairs, even after her hair grew back after chemotherapy.

She liked to spend time with her family. We took vacations together—all five of us in a camping trailer. We were a family of readers and talkers. We always ate supper together if at all possible and talked about our day. She loved music, and I grew up listening to show tunes on her record player. I can sing along with many more Broadway shows than my friends.

We loved to bake a variety of cookies each year at Christmas. My favorite kind was sand tarts. It was a time consuming process, requiring a few hours of chilling in the refrigerator, but the results were so worth it.

My mother made comfort foods. We used very few con-
venience foods. We usually had spaghetti, mac and cheese, pot
pie, beef roasts, pork and sauerkraut. We would try new foods,
especially after we had tried something new on vacation; after
a trip south, we had grits on a regular basis.

Cooking and nutrition were important to her, but fancy
food was not. She felt everyone should eat well. In fact, she
started Meals On Wheels in our town. I helped with that
when possible.   ❧ *Beth Bigler*

❧

My mother was very hard working, getting up early
every morning to make certain my dad had breakfast
before he headed out to milk the cows, and from then on,
she was one busy lady.

She often helped milk the cows, feed the calves, did the
milk separating, washed everything afterward, got me off to
school (sometimes she would take me on the tractor), worked
in the garden, fed the chickens, gathered the eggs, helped in
the field, and went on like this all day.

But there was still time for me to sit by her when she
played the piano. Sometimes I would sit beside her, and she
would rub my feet—and then start tickling them.

On Saturdays, especially if we had company coming,
we would clean the house from top to bottom. After Mom
mopped the dining room floor, I would get down on all fours
and wax the floor using a rag. When we were finished, we
would stand back and look for spots I had missed. I don't
know why I remember this so well, but I do!

She was a fantastic cook—the best in the family—and
our big family of aunts and uncles and cousins would often
be at our home for the holiday dinners. I always helped with
the cooking, which I learned at a young age, but what was

most special for me was getting to set the table with all her prized china and silver and pretty little pickle dishes and such.

Margie Huff Yongue

Boiled Raisin Cake
Doris [Coates] Huff

I copied the recipe exactly how I found it in her recipe box. I added info in brackets.

This was a family favorite but, however, not mine since I disliked cooked raisins but I loved the frosting and would sneak a piece off of the frosting whenever possible.

1. Boil 2 cups raisins in 1 cup water until water has boiled away. Add another cup of water and set off stove to cool.
2. ½ c. lard [or shortening], a level Tbsp of [baking] soda, 1 cup sugar, 1 Tbsp. cinnamon, salt [¾ tsp. salt], a little candied peel and flour [2 cups flour] to make regular cake batter. Brown sugar is better than white. Add nuts if desired.
3. I don't know exactly what she baked it at but I'm thinking 350° for about 30 minutes in a 9" pan until a toothpick would come out clean when pushed into the cake or when you touched the cake and it sprang back. Mom frosted this with a Browned Butter Frosting.

My mom was dressed well and nicely groomed. She moved and spoke with confidence, which is remarkable because she grew up in a difficult home with little encouragement from her parents.

She was our champion, standing up for her kids, and instilling in us confidence and the steadfast knowledge that we were beloved. Though her parental role models were not very helpful as references, she tried hard to be the best mom she could be.

She was skinny and underfed as a child but grew into a graceful and slim young adult, keeping her figure for decades. My mom was the only one of my friends' mothers who looked stylish in a bikini!

Later, when she became plumper, she faced the facts frankly and ate less and exercised more until she was happy again with how she looked. Her sweet tooth has never gotten the best of her—and she taught us kids to enjoy a taste of everything!

Our home was always filled with my and my siblings' friends, and it was always neat and inviting, and there were plenty of snacks or an extra place at the table. Friends told me, "Your

Linda Davis Siess' mother, Mimi, on the left with a friend in 1955 enjoying the sunshine and watermelon. Linda guesses they were having a seed-spitting contest, something Linda's mother told her not to do!

mom is cool!" When I told her that, she beamed and said that had been her dream when she was young and trying to rise above her dysfunctional family: that one day she would have kids and a home that they could be proud of.

🌶 *Linda Davis Siess*

My mother was a stay-at-home mother until my sister and I were in junior high and my younger sister and my brother were still in grade school. She went back to college and obtained her Masters of Library Science. She was the head librarian for Herron School of Art here in Indiana for many years.

When she began going to college, we began having to cook suppers for our Papa and us four children. It was the beginning of my culinary journey.

She and Papa always had a very big garden when we were growing up and after they retired. Mom loves all kinds of vegetables, and since Papa died in 2009, she has eaten less and less meat. She manages the family's sixty-nine-acre farm by herself at the young age of 83. Her house and garden are immaculately maintained, with the gardens around the house looking like a park.

She's fearless. When she was awakened in the middle of the night by her dog barking and frantically trying to get outside to get something or someone, she went outside with a pistol in the pocket of her robe to find that the cows had gotten one of the barnyard gates open. Those fearless genes were some I did not inherit.   ✺ *Cindy Latty*

Baked Apple Hand Pies

(or "Pies with Lids" as her grandson Matt
calls them—and now we all call them that)
Cindy Latty • *Makes 24-30 hand pies*

½ gallon dried apple slices

1-1½ cups sugar

1½ tsp. cinnamon

½-¾ tsp. nutmeg

Pie dough:

4 cups flour, plus additional
   for rolling out dough

½ tsp. salt

1⅓ cups butter-flavored
   shortening

13-14 tablespoons ice
   water

cinnamon and sugar
   mixture to dust the pies

*Cindy's son Matt, her mom
and her dog, Mollie in 2009.*

1. Put dried apples in large sauce pan. Add water to the apples until the water level is just barely visible below the apples (approx. 2 cups).

2. Simmer covered on medium low heat for approximately 1 hour, periodically adding more water (about 1" of water each time) until the apples are fully reconstituted, taking the lid off for the last 30 minutes.

3. Occasionally stir and chop the apples while they cook. After the apples are fully reconstituted, let the water almost completely cook away, watching the apples carefully. (If you allow too much water to remain with the apples, the pies will get soggy).

4. Stir in the sugar, cinnamon and nutmeg until you're satisfied with the taste.

5. Use a hand beater or electric mixer to completely cut up and incorporate the apples and spices. Set aside and let the apple mixture completely cool for several hours.

6. When the apple mixture is cooled completely, make the pie dough. Put the 4 cups flour into a large bowl.

7. Cut shortening into the flour using a pastry blender until the flour is similar to crumbly cornmeal.

8. Add the ice water one tablespoon at a time, lightly mixing the flour mixture with a fork until the mixture forms a ball in the bowl. Do not mix too much.

9. Sprinkle additional flour on your countertop or pastry board. Pinch off golf-ball-sized pieces of pie dough and quickly and lightly roll out the dough on the floured countertop using a floured rolling pin. Roll the dough into a small circle (about hand-sized in diameter) and about ⅛" thickness.

10. Set that rolled-out circle aside and pinch off another piece of dough, continuing to pinch and roll out the circles until you have all the dough rolled out into small circles.

11. Scoop about ¼ cup of cooled apple mixture onto a dough circle towards one side, leaving enough room around the edge for crimping.

12. Wet around the edge of the dough with a fingertip dipped in water. Fold the other edge of the dough circle over the apple mixture to make a half-moon shape. Crimp the edges together using a fork dipped in flour. Using that same fork, lightly poke once or twice into the top of the pie to allow steam to escape during baking.

13. Place the filled pie onto a lightly greased cookie sheet.

14. Continue to fill, crimp, and poke all the pies until all the dough is used (you may have extra apple mixture left over).
15. Dust each pie with the cinnamon sugar mixture.
16. Bake the pies at 350° until the pies are slightly browned and sound hollow when you lightly tap them, about 35 minutes. Let cool.

❧

S he was an extremely attractive woman and always wore Revlon Love That Red lipstick (I think that was *the* shade of the '50s!).

My mom was very active in Women's Club and the Pink Ladies (hospital auxiliary)—one of the ladies slim enough to wear a pinafore instead of a shapeless jacket like they all wear now. Volunteering was very important to her. She just wasn't a housewife type. In an era when a working wife was a sign that the husband wasn't capable of supporting his wife, I guess she channeled her desire to have a career into volunteering.

My mom wasn't much of a cook. Dinner was TV dinners and frozen foods, which were all the rage in the 1950s. Dinner was always on a rotation schedule. I believe she picked that up from my grandma who came from Germany. Every Tuesday was pork chop night. You always knew what was for dinner by what day of the week it was. It's too bad my mom passed away in 1972 because she would have been a *huge* fan of the slow cooker! ❧ *Mollie Dosch*

❧

M y mom is a little bird of a woman. But she's got a tiger inside.

She grew up on the edge of town with one sister, five years older. Things were clean and tidy. Then she married my dad, who grew up on a farm about two hours away, with his seven siblings and their schoolteacher parents.

Phyllis' mother, Betty Pellman, probably in the spring of 1947, said that the best lilacs were at the top of the bush!

My mom didn't know much about cooking when she got married. I'm guessing she wasn't that interested, plus my grandma was a great cook, and she moved around the kitchen as easily as she breathed. She baked cookies for the bi-weekly farmers market and had her routine down. I think it was one of those I-can-do-it-faster-myself situations. So when Ma married, she went digging through cookbooks.

Then my dad's sibs started dropping into their apartment, unannounced. She loved the company, but she learned fast that she needed to have a full fridge all the time. And then she learned that she needed to put signs on the bowls that were meant for other occasions than hungry kid brothers.

Recently, Ma was dipping into her diaries. "Wow," she said. "How'd I manage to do all that when I didn't really know how to cook?"

The same way she met all the unexpected moments in her life. By marching straight through.

        🐦 *Phyllis Pellman Good*

My mom always looked so happy and relaxed in the kitchen. If a recipe didn't work out, she didn't get upset; she'd just say, "Now we have the opportunity to try again!" She loved to make oysters Rockefeller late at night for herself and Dad (I could smell them and would sneak downstairs for a taste! They never minded.).

She cooked a lot of seafood because we lived on the coast of Massachusetts, and Dad's best friend was a lobsterman. It was common to find broken lobsters or clams and fish in our sink when we got home from school. My mom would smile and say, "Let's create something new!" When we finished, she and I would sit down at the kitchen table and write out our new recipe.   ❧ *Brenda Morra*

> We always sat down together for dinner if possible. We talked about our days and shared one good thing and one not-so-good thing about our day.

❧

I remember going around telling my friends that my mom was Betty White. They had the same hairstyle, grin, and dimples. Still do. We went for many walks together—private time, she called it.

My mom liked to sew and cook. She would make her four girls matching clothes, just because she could. She tried teaching me to sew, but it didn't stick. What did stick were her lessons on how to make a meal out of what was available, what some now call cooking on the fly.

My mom made a lot of Hungarian food, as her parents and my father's parents were from Hungary. One thing I remember is she loved making bread from scratch; as it was rising, she would make a pot roast or casserole to go with it.

She had the patience of a saint when it came to letting us use the cookie press or cookie cutters. The cookies didn't always come out perfect like hers, but she said ours were the best.

❧ Kathy Workman

Chicken Paprikas

Kathy Workman
serves 4-6

4 Tbsp. shortening
1 Tbsp. sweet Hungarian paprika
1 tsp. black pepper
2 Tbsp. salt
4-5 lbs. chicken pieces
1½ cups water
½ pint sour cream

Dumplings:
3 eggs beaten
3 cups flour
1 Tbsp. salt
½ cup water

I did not like chicken very much growing up, but my favorite thing in the world that Mom made was Chicken Paprikas.

1. In a large Dutch oven, brown onion in shortening.
2. Add paprika, pepper, salt and chicken pieces. Brown 10 minutes.
3. Add water, cover, and let simmer slowly until tender.
4. Meanwhile, make the dumplings. Bring a pot of water to boil. Mix dumpling ingredients together and beat with a spoon. Drop by teaspoonful into boiling water. Cook about 10 minutes; drain and rinse with cold water.
5. Remove chicken from pot and set aside. Add sour cream to liquid in the pan and mix well.
6. Add rinsed, drained dumplings and arrange chicken pieces on top. Heat through and serve.

My mother had the prettiest natural red hair and such dewy skin. She was a little on the plump side, which babies loved. To them she was safe and cushy.

My mama loved to sing and to play her guitar and piano. My sister and I would sing along. Daddy played the harmonica. At church on Sundays, they were often called upon to sing. I loved to sing at home, but being adopted, I didn't inherit their talent. I was shy and couldn't carry a tune. My mother thought that I felt left out, and she surprised me with a tambourine. It was important to her for me to be included with my family on stage.

We didn't have a lot of money, and sometimes food seemed to be a luxury. Her salmon patties and fried potatoes were awesome. We didn't have to brag on her chili because she did that herself! ❧ *Jamie Wingard*

❧

My mother and daddy moved to "the country" when I was a baby. She was home all day and embraced all the aspects of small farm life.

We had a milk cow, and my mother made butter and whipped cream patties. My mother let me churn the butter with her Daisy Churn. She supervised while she was sewing or preparing dinner. I remember asking again and again as I churned, "Is it ready?" And she would say, "Not yet. Just a little more." Looking back, I see now that was her way of giving me something to do that was helpful for the family and also kept me busy for a long time. I have the churn now and the wooden butter molds on a shelf in my kitchen.

❧ *Connie Page*

❧

Mom helped my friend and me put together a Halloween party with punch. No one showed up, but my mom was there. Sometimes that is all you need—your mom to be there.   ❧ *Joetta Russell*

❧

My mom was a loving and generous person. She enjoyed cooking, cleaning, and gardening and truly embraced her role as chief cook and bottle washer. I think this was in part because she never learned to drive, and my dad worked at nights, so our home was literally the center of her world. Mother Theresa once said, "Do small things with great love." That is exactly what my mom did her entire life.

I can vividly recall the times Mom would make lemon meringue pie. It was my dad's favorite, so she made it often. As a youngster, I remember helping her make the pie crust. I loved to roll out the dough on the old wooden pastry board with the worn wooden red-handled rolling pin. I was probably more hindrance than help, but she never made me feel that way. Then Mom would prepare the filling on the stove with egg yolks, sugar, and cornstarch.

More importantly, my mom taught me how to be kind and generous when she left a lot of the lemon pudding on the sides and bottom of the pan so I could clean it with the scraper and eat what was left.

My mom was also an avid gardener. The windowsills in our home were so covered with houseplants it was like a jungle. I often helped with transplanting and propagating. Mom died from cancer three months before my wedding when she was only 51. In her honor, I divided the plants and used them as centerpieces for our wedding reception. I still have some of those plants and that was thirty-five years ago, so I guess you could say they are antique houseplants.

Rose C. Speicher (right) with her mom and younger sister Michele in their yard, Easter 1959.

My mom was from a rural farming family, and my dad was from an Italian immigrant family that owned a produce company, which had its genesis from their own gardens. I suppose it was inevitable that I would enjoy cooking and gardening. When parents share their own interests with their children, they may be planting the seeds for life-long skills and treasured childhood memories. ❧ *Rose C. Speicher*

Lemon Meringue Pie
Rose C. Speicher

For pie filling:
2.75-oz. package My-T-Fine Lemon pudding and
pie filling (do not use instant pudding)
½ cup sugar
2¼ cups water, *divided*, may replace 2 Tbsp.
water with 2 Tbsp fresh lemon juice (I prefer
Meyer lemons)

My mom always used the recipe on the back of the pudding and pie filling box and she insisted it had to be the My-T-Fine brand. I have tried it with other brands and have to admit I prefer My-T-Fine, too! It's hard to find these days but can be ordered off the Internet; it's worth it to me just because using it reminds me of my dear mom who is no longer with us. It's amazing how recipes and certain foods trigger cherished memories of those we love.

2 egg yolks
8- or 9-inch pie crust, prebaked (my mom made her own but I cheat and use frozen storebought)

For meringue:
2 egg whites
¼ tsp cream of tartar
¼ cup sugar

1. Mix the contents of the lemon pudding and pie filling package with ½ cup of sugar and ¼ cup of water.
2. Stir in 2 egg yolks and 2 cups of water.
3. Cook over medium heat, stirring constantly until mixture comes to a full bubbling boil. Cool 5 minutes, stirring twice.
4. Pour into 8 or 9-inch cooled baked pie crust.
5. Prepare the meringue. Beat 2 egg whites and ¼ teaspoon of cream of tartar until foamy. Gradually beat in ¼ cup of sugar, beating until soft peaks form.
6. Spread meringue over the hot pie filling, sealing well to crust.
7. Bake at 350° for 10 to 12 minutes or until light brown. Cool to room temperature.
8. Refrigerate 3-4 hours before serving. Delicious with a cup of Earl Grey tea!

W̲e moved a lot from coast to coast because of my dad being in the Navy throughout my growing up years. Mom was always ready to pack up and move the whole family across the United States, at times even buying and selling homes by herself because Dad was overseas.

Every day, Mom would have supper on the table, right on time. She shopped for a month—even froze milk! Towards the end of the month, the pantry supply was getting down because Mom shopped once a month when Dad was paid.

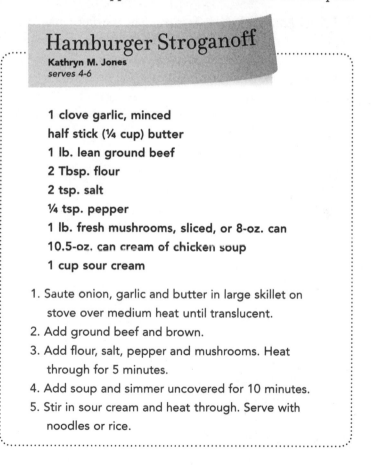

Hamburger Stroganoff

Kathryn M. Jones
serves 4-6

1 clove garlic, minced
half stick (¼ cup) butter
1 lb. lean ground beef
2 Tbsp. flour
2 tsp. salt
¼ tsp. pepper
1 lb. fresh mushrooms, sliced, or 8-oz. can
10.5-oz. can cream of chicken soup
1 cup sour cream

1. Saute onion, garlic and butter in large skillet on stove over medium heat until translucent.
2. Add ground beef and brown.
3. Add flour, salt, pepper and mushrooms. Heat through for 5 minutes.
4. Add soup and simmer uncovered for 10 minutes.
5. Stir in sour cream and heat through. Serve with noodles or rice.

One time the flour had bugs in it. Mom made soup with the flour anyway. There were all the flour weevils—in our soup. Dad said, "Eat it. Extra protein! If I can eat this on the ship, you can too!"

We always had a hot meal on the table daily, cleaned and pressed clothes, and a warm and inviting home when we got home from school—her energy was endless!

❧ *Kathryn M. Jones*

❧

We were an Amish family. My mother's name was Emma, and she was born in 1900. She was married to my dad, who was seven years older than she. She was kind, soft-spoken, and slow but steady. I recall no spankings from her. She liked to fry mush for our breakfast.

My maternal grandfather purchased our farm for his daughter and family. It appeared she was the neck that turned the head in business matters in a way that my father was not aware of. She and I milked cows by hand at the same time.

She was fancy in dress (the bishop came to see Father about this). Later my mother looked "spiffy" in dress because she and Father changed to a more liberal Mennonite church.

❧ *Esther J. Yoder*

❧

I wish to honor my mother-in-law whom I knew for a brief two years and nine months. She was already in her early sixties and looked like an angel with her halo of white braids tucked around her head. Each evening she would unbraid and brush out her long tresses.

She married young, had a son, and then her husband left her. She struggled terribly before she met my father-in-law who also had a son and had lost his wife in the 1917 flu epidemic. They married, and about twenty years later my husband was born—a surprise as she was already 42 and the doctor diagnosed her "condition" as a tumor! Living through the Great Depression and the struggle of being a single mom didn't dim her wit, humor, and loving nature.

While I was away at college, I was fortunate to spend weekends at my future mother-in-law's home. She welcomed me from the first moment I met her. When I went back to college near my birthday, she surprised me with a wonderful homemade cake to take with me and share with my college friends. No cake mixes for her!

I also spent two weeks with her when I was diagnosed with mononucleosis and the doctor would not permit me

French Dressing
Carol Findling

1½ Tbsp. salt
1 Tbsp. paprika
1½ Tbsp. dry mustard
1½ Tbsp. Worcestershire sauce
2 cups salad oil
1 cup vinegar, apple cider is
    good
1 cup tomato paste

1. Blend until well mixed. Store in the refrigerator. Drop in 1 garlic clove, punctured with a fork. Can be removed after a few days if desired.

This is one of the few recipes I have kept and comes from her mom, Grandma Renata Findling. It is great over vegetable salads and fruit salads, especially a spinach/strawberry/sesame seed salad.

to travel or go back to college. She fed me wonderful soups and especially, on the doctor's orders, meat cooked very rare. I was supposed to eat the drippings, too! Her bread worked wonders as a sponge to get every last drop. During this time, she shared old photographs of her parents and their many travels, especially to Florida and California. She was my hovering angel, and she was determined to get me well.

❧ Carol Findling

❧

My mom loved to make fried pies from her father's recipe. He sold them for a living and actually paid the doctor for delivering her with fried pies. (I have a copy of his journal where he recorded the transaction.) She cut the dough with the edge of a saucer like he used to do at his shop.

❧ Gloria Schratwieser

❧

My mother, a beautiful person, was repeatedly compared to Farrah Fawcett in the '70s. She was a 5'7" tall, blonde, green-eyed, somewhat shy, and very active woman. So many times, our mother was mistaken as our sister. Some of my favorite memories of her from when I was small are of her blushing face. She was teased about blushing, which only made her blush more and remain quiet. As she grew in her career into administrative positions, she became less shy, and when she received a degree in education and became a high school teacher, her shyness pretty much disappeared.

Mom was someone who encouraged healthy eating and meals that others in our area were unfamiliar with. We lived in southeast Ohio in a somewhat small college town. Most of the kids I went to school with had no idea what a pomegranate was, a kiwi, bean sprouts, not even an eggplant. Of course, times have changed since the '70s, and these items are more well known now.

Mom was someone who discouraged packaged foods. Even after I had children she would warn me not to permit them to eat high-sodium packaged noodles. Healthy eating has passed to each generation of our family, thanks to my mother. Not only have my sister and I always liked vegetable and fruit dishes, but my children and grandchildren prefer them over sweets.   ❧ *Tammy Johnson*

❧

My mom grew up on a dairy farm, and as a girl, spent a lot of time helping Grandpa out in the barn. She was also very interested in nursing, and as a young adult, she volunteered as a candy striper at a local hospital. I think she would have made a good nurse and would have enjoyed that career, but she never pursued it.

By the time I came along, the fourth daughter, she was pretty well established in her "career" as a farm wife. I don't remember her spending much time sitting still. She worked hard milking cows and mowing the yard (this was a job that most farm wives and farm kids did), and she had a huge garden. In her "spare time," she enjoyed sewing.

We didn't eat fancy meals but good, hearty, meat-and-potato type meals. We would often have families home from church for Sunday dinner. Since we grew up on a farm, we were able to eat most meals together as a family, especially in the summertime.

I remember that Mom would get us out of bed sometimes by calling up the steps,

One favorite recipe that Mom still makes is her baked corn.

"Grits for breakfast!" This was our favorite breakfast food.

Even though she's getting older, she still enjoys cooking for the whole family at holidays, although she is beginning to let us bring things to contribute to the meals.

Alica Denlinger

Baked Corn
Alica Denlinger

3 Tbsp. melted margarine
¼-½ tsp. salt
2 tsp. sugar
1 Tbsp. flour
2 eggs
1 cup milk

1. Place all ingredients in blender. Blend briefly until well mixed, stopping to stir and scrape down sides as needed.
2. Pour into greased 1½- or 2-quart casserole dish.
3. Bake at 350° for 35-40 minutes, or until center is firm.

Mom came to America from Hamburg, Germany, in 1955. She came with my father and older sister. They didn't have much money and worked hard for everything. Mom wasn't big on fashion—there was no money for it—but until her divorce, I don't ever remember Mom wearing pants. It just wasn't done by women her age back then.

My older sister "Americanized" Mom after her divorce. She started to wear pants and make up and had her hair cut and done on a regular basis.

Mom regularly made chili for us. It was cheap, and we loved it. Some of her other dishes that became family favorites were her potato pancakes, potato salad, sauerbraten, meatloaf, and rouladen.

A lot of special times with Mom were spent around the kitchen table, talking, and listening to Mom's stories about growing up in Germany, especially during World War II. Money was tight, so we didn't go to a lot of places that cost money. If we went to the German deli, we'd have to take a bus. And, if we got a special treat, we had to walk home from there, because there wasn't money for bus fare, too. We walked a lot, since Mom never owned a car.

> One summer it had been really hot, and we asked her if we could just have cold sandwiches for dinner. She enjoyed the sandwiches, since she didn't have to make a full dinner and heat up the house even more.

🍃 *Chris Lawenstein*

My mom grew up not having much, so she learned how to make things last. She could make our Thanksgiving leftovers go on forever. When there was nothing left but the bones, she would boil them and make the best soup you ever put in your mouth. If we had cornbread left after supper, she would turn it into what they called Hope Cake when she was a child. She would melt butter and pour it over the cornbread and then pour syrup on top. It was so good.

Her fried chicken was so good. If we had leftovers and knew someone that was sick or just alone, we would take it to them. I am so thankful she taught me how to give.

🍃 *Marie Anderson*

As far back as I remember, I was right there in the kitchen helping my mom. I was an only child, and my dad called me Little Mary after my mother. She was the mother who had treats ready for the neighborhood children. She helped me set up tea parties and lemonade stands.

My father had a barber shop in our home, so we often found customers having supper with us. When dinner was ready, Mother would call Dad, and if he wasn't too busy, his customers would just join us. There was always room at her table. In fact, I am sure of several people who just "happened" to drop in at supper time.

The men especially liked when she would cook wild game for them. Rabbit, pheasant, and venison were some of her best meals. Her fried rabbit was excellent. I remember one meal in particular when one of my dad's customers joined us for rabbit and ate my favorite piece! Mother also had no problem cleaning the game or killing and cleaning chicken, for that matter. She once raised a few chickens of her own because "fresh, fat, and homegrown is always the best," she would say.

As I grew older and still lived at home, my mother and I would hurry home from work trying to beat the other one home. The prize for this race was that the first one home got to make supper!

One time mother entered a chicken pot pie contest sponsored by a local chicken company after being persuaded to enter by many of those who had tasted her chicken pot pie. She became a finalist and appeared on WGAL TV in Lancaster, PA. We were all very proud of her.

To this day when I'm asked what my favorite food is, I always say her chicken pot pie. I have her pie board, her rolling pin, apron, and recipe, but my pot pie will never be as good as Mamma's was. I guess it was her special brand of love and a full house to share it with that made her pot pie just the best there ever was.   ❧ *Susan J. Heil*

Boiled Chicken Pot-Pie

Susan J. Heil
serves 4-6

3 quarts water
2 tsp. salt
1 tsp. parsley flakes
¼ tsp. pure Spanish saffron
3 cups all-purpose white flour
3 eggs
6 Tbsp. milk
black pepper, to taste
5 medium white potatoes, peeled
    and quartered
fresh parsley

My mother never used a recipe when she made it. She just needed to "feel it" and knew when it was right!

1. Using a 5 qt. saucepan, boil the chicken parts in the water seasoned with the salt. When the chicken is tender, remove and bone the chicken. Set aside.
2. Remove excess fat from the broth. Remove 2 cups of broth from the pan and put the boned chicken pieces into it. Keep warm.
3. Into remaining broth in saucepan, add parsley flakes and saffron.
4. Into a 2 qt. mixing bowl put the flour. Into a smaller bowl put the eggs and milk. Mix slightly. Pour the egg mixture into the bowl with the flour. Mix with a table fork. When thoroughly mixed, form the dough into a soft ball.
5. Taking the dough ball, roll it flat on a well-floured pie board until the dough is about 1/4 inch thick.
6. Sprinkle the dough with pepper and then roll over dough again lightly.

7. Cut the dough into 2-inch squares. Drop each
   square individually into rapidly boiling broth in the
   pot.
8. Add quartered potatoes. Simmer 45 minutes or
   until squares are soft and puffy and the potatoes
   are tender.
9. Turn into serving dishes, putting chicken pieces
   and broth on the top of the pot-pie squares and
   potatoes. Garnish with a fresh parsley sprig. This is
   excellent served with brown-butter peas and chow
   chow. If you like, simply drizzle brown butter over
   the whole dish.

❧

My father was in the military, and we moved around a lot. It was important to Mom to make our home, wherever it was, into a warm, attractive, welcoming place.

In our travels, Mom and Dad made a point of experiencing the culture and cuisine of the area we were living in and of learning recipes from our military friends from other lands. My friends would eat hamburgers or hotdogs for dinner, while we would eat Panang Curry or Weinerschnitzel. Mom made cooking these meals into a sort of social studies lesson. My brother, sister, and I would have to look up where the country was, what language was spoken there, and any interesting trivia we could find. We would then share this information at the dinner table. This evolved into the International Night that I do with my own children.   ❧ *Donika Engstrom*

❧

My mom may have only gone to school through the third grade and lived the life of a sharecropper's daughter, but she took care to look presentable everywhere she went. Even though she worked in the textile mills in Columbus, she still wore her lipstick. I still remember watching her apply her favorite lipstick, Cherries In the Snow. While fighting breast cancer in her late thirties until she lost all of her hair and had to wear wigs, she still was careful to look the best she could until she lost the battle at age 47. I was 16, and I knew how hard she fought to survive.

Although my mom did not have a strong educational background, she was smart in so many ways. She taught herself to sew by taking old clothes apart and making patterns for new ones. One day I came home from school, and she had made an entire wardrobe for my Barbie dolls, including a winter coat! Later as she became disabled, she took a knitting class with my older sister and produced some family heirlooms we still cherish to this day.

My mom did the cooking most of the time, but my dad was a ship's cook in the Navy during World War II, so he took over on Sunday mornings. He really had to take over once my mom got sick. We all sat down together, and the blessing was said first before anyone took a single bite. I remember always having fresh vegetables at most of our meals, and I grew up liking them all. Sometimes all we ate were vegetables, and I did not miss the meat.   ❧ *Kathy Ausburn*

❧

My father was a Mennonite minister and also a farmer. Consequently, my mother was a very busy woman. She had a big garden and preserved a lot of food. She kept the big farmhouse clean and tidy.

She dressed in plain Mennonite garb and always wore an

apron at home. There was always a clean apron hanging on a hook nearby in case someone stopped in. I clearly remember her quickly pulling off the apron she was wearing and slipping on the clean one if someone came to the door. Appearances were important to her.

She was a very good cook, especially as it applied to typical farmer's fare. She made wonderful puddings and desserts, a regular at our meals.

I recall that after meals it was my job to "redd" off the table and then dry the dishes as my mother washed. Even though I resented having to do these chores when my brothers could go dashing outdoors after meals, I remember these times as a good time to talk.

Scalloped Salmon
Esther Becker

I don't have a recipe for this dish but here is how I remember it. My mother loved this dish and made it often; my children came to expect it if they were going to Grandma's house!

1-2 sleeves saltines, crumbled
14-oz. can salmon
2 eggs
milk to cover crackers
butter

1. Place half of the cracker crumbs in bottom of greased 1½ qt. baking dish. Layer half of the salmon over crackers. Repeat layers, saving a few cracker crumbs for the top.
2. Beat eggs, pour over crackers and salmon, then add milk to fill to top of dish. Dot with butter. Sprinkle with reserved crumbs.
3. Bake at 350° for 35 minutes.

One time when we were doing dishes together, she washing and me drying, she told me we were going to have a new baby. I was quite surprised and had some questions but was too shy to ask them. It felt good to me that she had shared the news with me. I felt sort of grown up. ❧ *Esther Becker*

❧

M om loved reading and cooking and was a compulsive cleaner—never walked by a surface anywhere that she didn't wipe with a tissue or her hand, including my face.

She was happiest taking us places to play and enjoy ourselves. We camped, which looking back I don't think she enjoyed all that well because there is just no way to wipe down the outdoors. Oh, we had so much fun! She was really a little kid at heart.

The most important thing in her life was being a mother. I know a lot of people say that, but she was special because she wasn't able to have birth children and waited patiently while suffering inside for years to adopt her two children. She truly viewed being a mother as her greatest achievement in her life.

Her cooking was the typical early 1960s fare—casseroles, meat, and lots of gravy, anything you can find in a typical diner. Lots of fat and salt, and it was delicious.

❧ *Denise Portelance*

❧

M om had scrunchy Toni perms that her sister or her friend would give her in the kitchen, making the house smell so bad that none of the men would come inside until the process was over. She'd set all those fuzzy hairs in bobby pins and then wrap a bandana around it all until it dried. She's been gone twenty-five years, but her smile lingers in the memory bank of my heart.

Because my dad worked nights and I worked days, she usually had all four burners of the stove going on a Saturday morning. One burner would be for chili con carne, another for vegetable soup, another might be ham and green beans, and yet another chicken pot pie. In this way, she'd have a hot meal for us at whatever time of the day we were eating. She always, always sat down to share the meal with us, even if she only had a cup of coffee herself.

She possessed a great deal of wisdom and taught me from a very early age to be busy with my hands and to take care of my husband and family. And to make our home one with an open door, almost a revolving door. I haven't counted how many people actually moved in with us during hard times. She kept the coffee pot going and put a sign in the window of the kitchen: "Eva's Coffee Shop—Bring your own donuts."

Another nugget of wisdom she passed on was to always go with your husband when he wants to go somewhere. You don't have to completely love the place, but there are plenty of women who are out there looking for a man like yours, and they'd be more than happy to take him off your hands for you.

When I got engaged, she told me it was time I learned how to cook.

One particular day she was making fried chicken. I might add that I never ate chicken until I was 21, and then I covered the uneaten portion with a napkin because it looked so disgusting to me. She had filled up half of the sink with water and had chicken pieces floating around doing the backstroke. Her instructions were to pick up each piece and make sure there were no pin feathers in the piece. "Your father hates pin feathers." Really, I could not bring myself to reach into that tepid water and retrieve a wet, naked, bumpy piece of dead chicken. In frustration, she grabbed a piece and slapped it into my hand. I screamed and pitched the chicken straight up where it bounced off the ceiling! My cooking lesson was done—the only one I ever got. 🦌 *Ginny Walls*

🌿

Mom made some pretty exotic dishes by today's standards, like sweetbreads and kidney stew! She loved to make padded fried oysters, pineapple upside-down cake, bread pudding, and pies. She said she'd rather make ten pies than one cake because when you bake a cake you still have to frost it! She made great chili, wonderful sauerbraten with gingersnap gravy, and terrific pot roasts. 🦌 *Mary Puskar*

Pineapple Torte
Mary Puskar

1½ tsp. vanilla
1 tsp. vinegar
2 cups sugar
1 cup crushed pineapple, drained
¾ cup maraschino cherries, quartered,
    plus some whole ones for garnish
2 cups heavy cream, whipped

1. Bring egg whites to room temperature. Add vanilla and vinegar and beat until mixture forms soft peaks.
2. Add sifted sugar, 1 tablespoon at a time. Continue beating until very stiff and all sugar is dissolved.

She made a dessert called a Pineapple Torte. It was not easy to make and I have only made it once.

This is as light as a feather and so good.

3. Spread into two 9" cake pans which have been lined with heavy brown paper around the sides and bottom. You want the paper to stand up above the sides.
4. Bake in a slow oven, 300°, for one hour and fifteen minutes. Turn oven off. Let cool in oven one hour.
5. Add pineapple and cherries to whipped cream and spread between the layers of the cake as well as on the top and sides.
6. Garnish with whole cherries. Chill 12 hours before serving.

My mom and dad married when she was 14 and Daddy was 21. I asked her once if she regretted getting married so young, and she told me she never had a childhood, and she should have waited. Their firstborn died about a month after he was born. One was born in Texas, and the other five of us were born in Oklahoma during the hard times. We all grew up about ten miles out in the country, and everyone was poor out there. We chopped cotton and then pulled cotton just to get by.

Momma would fill every container she had, and on a pretty day, she would set the tubs up and proceed to do the wash. Momma was 75 when she got her first clothes dryer.

Momma had a garden in the summer and canned, so that is what we ate most of the time. I don't even think my mom had a cookbook. Momma made Poor Man's Pudding a lot. I know it had day-old homemade bread in it, but I don't know what else.

We always had a cow for milk. I think I was in high school when I had my first glass of iced tea.   ❧ *Joy Goade Zowie*

꙰

I grew up in an affluent suburb of New York City, where most of the mothers stayed home. They were fit and trim and were always showing up at the school in cute tennis outfits to do volunteer work. My mother, on the other hand, worked as a teacher and then as a principal at a school for severely autistic children. She had no time for tennis, and I bemoaned her solid frame and decidedly un-cute fashion choices. Her priority, upon returning home from an undoubtedly challenging work day, was to cook the family meal. And cook she did. Her budget was limited, but she made wholesome, delicious fare for us every single night.

I have tried countless times, but I still cannot replicate her completely, utterly perfect roast chicken with vegetables. She always says, "Kate, it's simple. Salt the chicken well, put a lemon in the cavity, dab on some butter, put a bunch of carrots and onions around it, and stick it in the oven 'until it's ready.'" Ahh, maybe that's it—perhaps she has been blessed with the uncanny understanding of chicken readiness! She always serves her roast chicken with a simple, crisp green salad. Simple perfection!   ❧   *Kate Silverstein*

꙰

My mom is a very cheerful person. If I couldn't find her, I just had to hold still and listen for her cheerful whistling and then follow the sound until I found her. I don't remember Mom complaining or acting overwhelmed, although she may have felt like it at times. She would sing hymns in the grocery store, which my sister and I thought was super embarrassing.

Often she would come out our long lane to meet us with

a snack on our way home from school. One of my favorites was dough boys: bread dough shaped into a pancake and fried with butter and sugar on top. ❧ *Jan Byler*

❧

My mom had four lovely daughters who all looked like my dad. Dad was 6'4", and we were all tall and blonde. Everyone in town knew us as Russ Johnson's girls; only a few people knew she was our mom. She was a beautiful, tiny little brunette. She had piercing blue eyes that lit up when she was happy. Mom was a strong and determined person.

When I was young, Dad's business was attached to our house. Every evening at 6:00 Mom would wait by the kitchen door for Dad to come "home." She always greeted him with a smile, a hug, and a kiss. In return, my dad always cut a rose from the garden each morning for Mom to take with her to school.

When Mom was diagnosed with cancer and told she only had a month or two to live, she didn't give up. She continued to live life to the fullest, treating life as a precious gift that she could share with her family and friends. She knew that God still had plans for her, and she just kept plugging along. Twelve years later, she started a cancer support group in our town.

We loved spending time together in the kitchen. She was always showing me an easier, better, or quicker way to do things or some new recipe she wanted to try. She would tell us stories about her life growing up in a cabin in northern Idaho as we cooked up a holiday feast. She made it seem magical. ❧ *Becky McClees*

Meatloaf
Becky McClees

1 lb. hamburger
1 lb. ground pork
¼ cup quick oats
1 egg
¼ cup ketchup, plus extra
sliced pickles
4 slices bacon
sliced cheddar cheese

1. Mix together the ground meats, oatmeal, egg, and ketchup.
2. Spread half of the mixture in a loaf pan. Cover with a layer each of ketchup, bacon, pickles, and cheese. Spread remaining meat mixture over the top.
3. Bake at 350° for 40 minutes or until done. Can be made ahead of time and refrigerated until time to bake.

⁖

My mom was one of three daughters of Amanda and Author, from Millersburg, PA. My mom's sisters were never blessed with children. I am an only child, so in essence I had three moms!

My mom and her sisters often disagreed on the way their mother prepared recipes. One would say, "Well, Mother added this ingredient!" Another would say, "No, she didn't!" I remember as a child listening to them cook together, laughing, disagreeing, and most of all passing down to me their mother's love of cooking for loved ones. ✦ *Susan Elmer*

As a history teacher in the early '50s, instead of being the usual stay-at-home mom, my mom was ahead of her time, and there was no support back then for women employed outside the home. A college degree plus a masters made her a rarity in that era.

My mom married later in life and adopted my twin sis and me. I think mothering twins was quite the shock to her as she was an only child of the Depression. Food must have been short in her childhood as meals were important and food was never wasted. After my dad was diagnosed with diabetes, she became even more concerned about our meals.

I remember how she'd spend summers off from teaching going to orchards to buy peaches, pears, plums, and tomatoes to can. Our next door neighbor had a huge pie cherry tree, and we canned pints and pints of them. I pitted many a cherry sitting at the kitchen table. Her life always seemed tied to food and us.

My mom always made us angel food cake topped with strawberries for our birthdays. I don't know the exact recipe she used, but I like to think it was from the *Betty Crocker Cookbook*; hers was as worn and stained as the one she gave me in 1966 when I married.

We rarely had sweets, and candy was allowed once a week; my sis once snooped in the candy box and found a note saying, "Have an apple instead!'

As soon as we were old enough, my sister and I were encouraged to take over cooking. We alternated days of cooking and cleaning up, our goal being to make as many dirty dishes as we could for each other! Looking back I believe my mother really didn't like cooking at all! ❧ *Diana Smith*

We never owned a home; we always rented. We didn't have the best of things, but we had a lot of love. My dad was a coal miner—that explains a lot.

My first weekly job was scrubbing kitchen chairs and baseboards. Then I was allowed to wash silverware but not sharp knives. I ironed handkerchiefs and, believe it or not, my dad's boxers.

My mom was an old-fashioned meat and potatoes cook, and she used fresh veggies from the garden. We had fruit trees in our yard. Sunday was the day family came for dinner, with homemade pies, cakes, and cookies for dessert.

We had to eat what she placed in front of us—no complaining. The only exception was liver and onions. She would make us kids something different. Thank you, Mom! I never had a hamburger on a bun until I was a teenager. Hamburger was our meat, with gravy made from the drippings and served over bread. Delicious!

Mom cooked everything on top of the stove. Meatloaf, roasts, halupkis—everything! That's one thing I've never been good at. I don't trust myself. I'm an oven or Crockpot cook.

❧ Bonnie Schoeneman

❦

My mother, Barbara Ebersole Brubaker, loved her Lancaster County kitchen, and it showed. Each day she put on a clean starched apron that matched her plain cape dress and wore it all day. She sewed a drawer-full of these full aprons from print cotton.

I remember that even her kitchen windows were well-dressed with fresh curtains for every season. Our kitchen and dining room tables likewise wore lovely tablecloths, fine china, and often roses and irises, which grew in our yard on Rose Avenue. Mother had a good eye for color and design and a creative spirit toward cooking. My children still have good memories of this short woman in the kitchen, smiling with pleasure, working with efficiency and a plan!

Mother's energy and highly-developed culinary skills served her well even in her teenage years. Although her formal education ended, as many girls' did then, in sixth grade, Mother had learned enough on the family farm before 1920 to go into Lancaster and work in the restaurant kitchen of the fine old Brunswick Hotel across from the train station.

Before dawn, she walked to the hotel where she baked about four dozen pies from scratch, before heading to her seamstress and tailoring classes. Later in the day, she returned to the hotel to shuck and prep oysters and clams for dinner guests. I know all this because as the oldest child, my mother and I washed and dried dishes together every evening—a lovely way to end the day's work, talking together about growing up.

It wasn't long before Mother's accomplishments were noticed by Jacob Engle Brubaker, who had been ordained as a minister at East Chestnut Street Mennonite Church in March 1918. Dad and Mother married in October the same year. Shortly thereafter, Mother's father and brothers helped them build the brick home on Rose Avenue, with careful attention to the kitchen, which had, and still has, windows on two walls where Mother grew African violets and geraniums on the sills, access to an enclosed back porch and the basement for storage, and a table in the middle.

Both Dad and Mother believed in having quality kitchen equipment. Dad bought her stainless steel pots and pans when they first became available. Mother had a Waring blender and a pedestal mixer. Once he brought home a roaster oven and in the 1970s, a Crockpot. As a couple, they enjoyed learning about new cooking techniques, new foods, and new flavors. Dad liked investing in new gadgets and the latest "technology." In his shop, he made wooden potato mashers, rolling pins, and salad bowls and even designed a string bean huller for her.

As a minister's wife, Mother was expected to be prepared to host an unknown quantity of Sunday dinner guests after the church service. Luckily, she had a true gift of hospitality that made visitors feel honored and special at any time. On Saturday, Dad would unnecessarily remind her to prepare plenty for Sunday; I think he took pride in anticipating the pleasure of sitting around the dining room table enjoying lively conversation with visitors and hearing them compliment the bountiful dishes.

At the dinner table in the Brubaker home in 1953: (left to right) Menno Fast, Naomi Brubaker Fast, Elisabeth Fast (1), Catherine Fast (3), Barbara Ebersole Brubaker, and Jacob Engle Brubaker.

Of course, this meant that while Dad was polishing his sermon on Saturday, Mother and I were in the kitchen cooking and baking. And of course the table was carefully set before we went to bed, with a couple of extra place settings. I clearly remember Mother saying many times, when all was ready, "Now, I've got my guns loaded!" It makes me smile still, to think of a Mennonite minister's wife loading her "guns" with mashed potatoes, pot roast of beef, roast chicken (never fried!), a pork roast, meat loaf, or ham.

She had vegetables from A (asparagus) to Z (zucchini), relishes, breads, jellies, chow-chow, dried corn, and perhaps our family favorite: an entire huge cauliflower head, steamed until tender in salted water, placed in a china serving dish, with a generous cup of glistening browned butter poured over top, shining like a golden jewel. For those who still had room, there was pie and coffee. There was lots of conversation. No one left the table early, not even children; it was an exciting place to be.   ✒ *Naomi Brubaker Fast*

✦

Mom grew up in the Ozarks and was able to go only to eighth grade in school. When she was 16, she was on her own, going to Kansas City to work in a soap factory, wrapping bars of soap. She and her sister had an apartment with some other girls.

While doing that, she met my dad who had recently returned from World War I. They rode the Interurban train from Kansas City to Lawrence and got married in the courthouse there. Since times were hard and jobs scarce, she and Dad traveled from coast to coast seeking work for Dad.

When my older brother was born in North Carolina, Dad bartered his painting skills for her care during his birth. About three years later, a second son was born in San Diego. When he was just a few weeks old, they traveled back to Kansas City in an old Model T Ford, camping along the way.

Mom always made the best of things and, as the old saying went, would use it up, wear it out, make it do, or do without. She recycled when that wasn't "in" and had the ability to make delicious meals from simple ingredients.

She made especially good fried chicken, which was probably the family favorite. Since we raised our own chickens, I learned early to go to the chicken yard, pick a likely candidate, decapitate it, scald, pick, and clean the chicken for her to fix for our dinner.

I remember when I was small, a coyote caught a chicken in the field. Mom yelled and ran to the scene, scaring the coyote away without his prey. Since the chicken was a goner, she butchered it and cleaned it, and we had chicken that night.

Another time, she was trying to scare a turkey away from the house and threw a rock at it. To her surprise, she hit it in the head, killing it. He later appeared on our table, giving us several good meals.

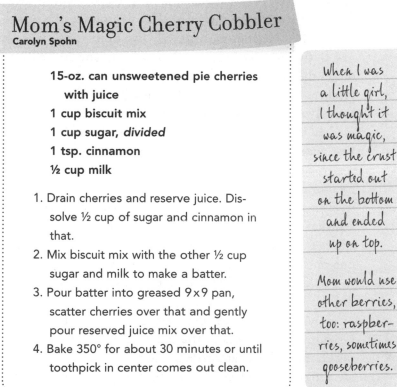

Mom's Magic Cherry Cobbler
Carolyn Spohn

> 15-oz. can unsweetened pie cherries
>   with juice
> 1 cup biscuit mix
> 1 cup sugar, *divided*
> 1 tsp. cinnamon
> ½ cup milk

1. Drain cherries and reserve juice. Dissolve ½ cup of sugar and cinnamon in that.
2. Mix biscuit mix with the other ½ cup sugar and milk to make a batter.
3. Pour batter into greased 9x9 pan, scatter cherries over that and gently pour reserved juice mix over that.
4. Bake 350° for about 30 minutes or until toothpick in center comes out clean.

When I was a little girl, I thought it was magic, since the crust started out on the bottom and ended up on top.

Mom would use other berries, too: raspberries, sometimes gooseberries.

Dad had coon dogs, and an elderly African-American gentleman he worked with came to our house to see the dogs. Mom made a very nice dinner and invited him and his friend to eat. Since that was in the '40s, he hesitated to eat at the table with us and said he would just have his dinner on the porch. Both of my parents would not hear of anything but us all sitting around the table together to eat. Even though I was just a little girl, I felt proud of my parents.

Carolyn Spohn

❧

M om always was up early and ready to greet us children when we woke up. If it was during the school year, we had to get up early to walk two miles to school each day. In the summertime, we often woke up and found Mom out in the garden picking our produce for the day or getting produce ready to take to Friday's market in New Holland, PA. My mom made our dad very proud.

My mom talks about the time when she and Dad were first married in the late '30s and food and money were very scarce. She and Dad hunted dandelions so they would have food to eat. She tells me they lived on dandelions for several weeks to save money for other needs. One day they found a nickel and were overjoyed at the sight. They decided to splurge and went to the local grocery store and bought one pint of ice cream to share and eat. She loves ice cream to this day but says that "none ever tastes as good as that did."

My grandmas were also very good cooks. I loved my Grandma Good's pies in the old-fashioned pie plates, and my Grandma Burkhart made the best shellbark cookies I ever ate. I'm sure this is where my mother learned her good cooking skills. And also why I always enjoyed cooking and trying new recipes.

We grew our own strawberries. One day, Mom finished making a large batch of homemade strawberry jelly, and the jars were all lined up on the kitchen counter to cool. She used paraffin wax to seal the jars. My youngest brother was 2 years old, and the rest of the children were in school. My mother

Grandma Burkhart's Shellbark Cookies

Jeanette Oberholtzer
Makes about 4 dozen cookies

¼ cup butter
¼ cup shortening or use ½ cup lard instead of
    shortening and butter
⅓ cup granulated sugar
⅓ cup light brown sugar
1 egg
1⅓ cups flour
¾ tsp. baking soda
¾ tsp. vanilla
⅓ cup finely chopped shellbarks

> *Shellbarks are a kind of hickory nut. Use walnuts instead if you wish.*

1. Melt shortenings and butter. Add sugars and mix well.
2. Add egg and beat till light.
3. Sift flour and baking soda and stir into shortening mixture.
4. Add vanilla and nuts.
5. Shape dough into rolls, 1½" in diameter. Roll in waxed paper and chill overnight.
6. Slice thin and bake on ungreased cookie sheet in 375° oven for about 10 minutes. *Do not overbake!*

went outside to do a quick chore, and when she came back in the house my little brother had climbed up onto the kitchen counter and pushed all the wax down into the jelly jars and was licking the jelly off his fingers and hands. There was jelly everywhere. I don't know what Mom's first thought was, but what she did was grab the camera and take pictures, so we could all enjoy the scene afterward. My brother was told what he did wrong, but he was not punished. My mom thought he was too young to understand why it was not a good idea.

Jeanette Oberholtzer

❧

My mom was a single mom, and we lived with my grandparents and aunt. My mom and aunt took turns by the week to cook. My mom liked to make pies—graham cracker crusts with a cooked pudding were one of her specialties. She also made chocolate shoofly pies. On the weekends, we would eat half of a shoofly pie for Saturday breakfast and save the other for Sunday breakfast. She also liked to make oven suppers, and she made the best scalloped potatoes. I liked when my mom cooked as she paid more attention to details and making things good than my aunt did.

We always had soup for Saturday lunch—often bean soup made with dried navy beans. At Christmas we would have oyster pie for breakfast—two crusts with oysters and milk as the filling. At Christmas there would be a plate at each place with candy and fruit. My mom always made fudge and puffed rice candy for our big Christmas get-together with my aunts and cousins. Her delicious sand tarts were also a Christmas necessity.

Rhoda Nissley

My aunt, grandma and mom are so closely intertwined in cooking that it is hard to always say who made what.

꤮

My mom's time in the kitchen was pretty much brought to a halt when we moved into a children's home the year I turned 7 so my parents could be the house parents. We had a cook. Her name was Mimi, and she was a sweet little German lady who wasn't at all intimidated by dinner for thirty every night. God bless her.

Mom's priority at that time became to raise the thirty kids who would come into our home over the next ten years to the honor and glory of God. It was great! Both of my parents were home full-time when I was growing up.

We did a lot of canning and freezing in the summer months when folks would drop off donations of produce. I remember getting up from rest time and being required to husk a truck load of corn before we could go swim in the pool. Or being covered in tomatoes as we strained them and made sauce and stewed tomatoes for hours. These kinds of chores became fun, and my mom was always the one with a game or a song to make the time and the task go quickly.

Some of the best times were the two-week vacations we'd take—just our family—to Ocean City, New Jersey, in the summer. I suppose then Mom would have to try to recall how to cook! She's always been creative though.

I think Mom's favorite thing to make (and one of her mom's favorite things to make) was fudge. We'd always have a batch on vacation. Even now when we go on vacation with the family as grown children with our own kiddos, Mom is sure to have fudge at the ready and has taught all the sons-in-law and my son to make it.   ❧ *Lisa Wolfe*

Fudge
Lisa Wolfe

My son makes it better than I do and it's one of his favorite things to do when we stay with Mom-mom on summer vacation or Christmas break.

2 cups sugar

3 heaping Tbsp. unsweetened cocoa

½ cup milk

1 Tbsp. butter, plus more for greasing
   the plate and pan

2 heaping Tbsp. peanut butter

2 Tbsp. marshmallow fluff

1 cap-full vanilla (maybe ¼ tsp.)

1. Mix sugar and cocoa together in a medium saucepan. Add milk and stir again until wet-looking over medium heat. Don't over-stir.
2. Meanwhile, butter a plate. Place the butter, peanut butter, marshmallow fluff, and vanilla on the plate. Set aside.
3. Prepare a wide glass of cold water and set aside. Butter a square baking pan and set aside.
4. When the mixture (fudge) in saucepan is at a rolling boil, doubles in size, and looks dark, stir ONCE to remove stuff from sides.
5. Take a teaspoon of fudge from saucepan and drizzle into cup of water. It should easily form a little ball with your fingers at the bottom of the glass. It's done. Remove from heat.
6. Add ingredients from plate and stir together.
7. Pour fudge into the buttered baking pan. Chill. Cut into squares. Enjoy!

I was an only child, so I spent many hours alone with my mom while I was growing up. Many of my memories center around the two of us in the kitchen.

I didn't realize until I was older that my mom wasn't actually very fond of cooking. She baked bread, cooked all our meals, even spent a long day each fall making enough mint tea concentrate for us to drink iced tea throughout the coming seasons, but she only did it out of a sense of duty.

She confessed to me that she never spent much time in the kitchen before she got married. She had older sisters who loved cooking and baking much more than she did. I was surprised at this confession, because I always thought she was a very good cook. I had no idea this wasn't one of her favorite activities.

One of her specialties was half moon pies. I particularly loved her crust. It was always very thin and flaky, which was why I was shocked when she admitted hating to make pie dough. "But your pie crust is so good!" I protested. "Well, I've perfected the recipe over the years so I can make large batches quickly," she explained.

It took me a while to recover from these revelations, and when I finally did, I could never look at my mom in the kitchen in quite the same way. I still enjoyed her food and continued to cook with her, but I seemed to do more of the cooking while she cleaned up after me. Now, many years after admitting her apathy towards cooking, my mom no longer "has" to cook. Surprisingly she seems to enjoy it much more.

Her cookbook collection has swelled to over a hundred cookbooks, and she's constantly clipping recipes from magazines. I love watching her learn to love cooking. It's taken nearly half a century, but I think my mom finally enjoys being in the kitchen! 🍃 *Bethanny Baumer*

My mom moved to New York City from a rural town in the Philippines. She told me that her first glimpse of snow was a disappointment because she thought it was white, not grey and brown. I remember her arriving home just in time to see me and my brother off to school. Her hair would be tousled after removing her hat (Mom never felt warm) after she got home from her twelve-hour overnight shift as a nurse.

On the days she was off work, she would forego sleep to make Filipino comfort foods. We would come home to deep pots of arroz caldo—a chicken and rice soup with hints of ginger served with a hard-boiled egg and a squeeze of lemon. Sometimes it was spaghetti made with a sweet homemade tomato sauce. She would watch us eat it while we talked about our day in school. ❧ *Michelle Pascua*

❧

My mother was pretty in spite of the plain cape dresses she wore because her church expected all women to dress that way. But as a child, I didn't know she was plain. What I knew was that if I needed to find her, she was usually in the kitchen—lingering over her breakfast coffee and reading the newspaper or ironing clothes. To this day, I love the smell of ironing.

Her favorite thing was cooking. Mostly she made roast beef and mashed potatoes, but she could cook anything. As a young woman, she had worked for wealthy people in Lancaster and Philadelphia as housemaid or cook. When my brother cleaned out some pigeon nests and

> My mother cooked lots of meals for people who were invited home from church. I always enjoyed everything from fruit salad appetizer to roast ham to cake and applesauce.

brought her the squabs, she knew how to clean and prepare them.

In February 1958, we had a blizzard so big it kept us home from school for a whole week. That week my mother made bread on at least two days. She made both plain white bread and cinnamon swirl. I thought the cinnamon swirl was pure magic.

Another time I specifically remember the food was on my wedding day. I was too excited to eat. She calmly prepared some sweet bologna sandwiches and coaxed me and my bridesmaids to eat. We stood at the kitchen counter chatting and enjoying my mother's blessing.　　　　*　*Elaine Good*

❧

My mom has Huntington's disease. This disease makes it so she can't be up like she used to. That does not mean that she can't be in the kitchen! She likes to sit in her wheelchair and watch me learn to cook. My "big sister" helps me learn to cook. She works with me. We bake cookies and cook casseroles.

I am 9 and still learning to cook. My mom tastes some of the food when we are baking. She used to like to bake cookies. It is important to her that I learn to clean up the kitchen. Even though she can't teach me to cook, she still likes being with me when I am learning.　　　　*　*Karissa Newswanger*

❧

My mom is short, has pretty brown eyes, a turned-up nose, and a cute crooked smile. Creativity flows through her veins whether it be in making lovely arrangements of her own cut flowers or running her sewing machine full tilt to make comforters and garments for those who have suffered misfortune.

Cooking is not as interesting to her, but I remember her concocting nice company meals. It was very special to eat Sunday morning breakfast using her pull-out kitchen cutting board for a table. The kitchen table was extended with all the boards and set with china for the company who were expected.

> Mom is a great believer in eating your fill of whatever vegetable happens to be in season, so we sometimes had asparagus twice a day.

She was skilled at making work into fun. If we were shelling hull peas, we'd race to see who could shell ten pods first or who could find the most peas in a pod. When she was ironing, she'd send us to make deliveries to various bedrooms upstairs. "Mrs. Smith lives in the second room on the right." On winter evenings, she often read to us.

Mom's walk with Jesus is very important to her. Being hospitable to strangers was an idea she modeled for us. When I was small, we would receive occasional visits from tramps (so named, I suppose, from tramping about from place to place) also known as hobos. They were homeless men who roamed the byways or illegally rode the train from one area to another looking for a meal or a little work. Mom always made them a nice breakfast. We children were shy and a little afraid of these, in our eyes, unusual men. She would tell us we might be entertaining angels unaware.

🐦 *Becky S. Frey*

🐦

My mom was a small woman (4'9¾"), and she wouldn't let you forget the three-quarter inch. She always wore an apron in the kitchen to keep anything from getting on her clothing. Mom always looked nice and had her hair done every couple of weeks with her "mad money."

Keeping a good home for my dad and me was important to her. She had a day for everything: laundry on Monday, ironing on Tuesday, cleaning on Wednesday, correspondence and bill paying on Thursday, grocery shopping on Friday, and the weekend was for spending time with Dad and me.

She made dozens and dozens of Christmas cookies. My dad took a whole big Crowley's gift box of them—multiple layers—to work at the plant. We gave them as Christmas gifts to neighbors and friends, and I always took some to school for the class.

Now my husband and I live in the home I grew up in, and when I'm in the kitchen, baking or cooking or making a cup of tea, I feel her spirit with me, and memories come flooding back. I hear things she used to say. I hear her songs. I miss my mom, but her legacy lives on in me through my cooking and baking. I would always rather make a meal at home than go out to eat, and I love to bake for my husband, friends, and co-workers.   *Pamela Conley*

❧

Mom was a quiet Mennonite lady, so we didn't talk much as we worked together. She didn't spend much time in the kitchen, but we had some rituals. Always, always, we mixed up a bowl of Jello on Saturday evening for Sunday dinner—just plain Jello, because we children liked it in its purest, uninvaded form!

And we peeled potatoes on Saturday evening for mashed or scalloped potatoes for our Sunday dinner. We needed to be prepared for company any time, because my dad was the talker of the two, and if there were visitors in church, he'd invite them home for dinner.

Other times that Mom spent in the kitchen were before we got home from school. It was the smell outside the door that told us of her special love for her hungry school children—oatmeal chocolate chip cookies all in rows on newspaper, plus the warm ones just out of the oven. Once a week, there was that unbeatable smell of fresh bread that came wafting down the lane when we walked in from the bus. It must have given her incentive to bake week after week to think ahead to our delight and her gratification when we'd burst in the door! ❧ *Marlene Graber*

Oatmeal Chocolate Chip Cookies
Marlene Graber

9 cups quick oats
4½ cups flour
3 cups brown sugar
3 tsp. baking soda
6 tsp. baking powder
3 cups milk (sour milk, chocolate milk, etc. were used also!)
3 eggs
2¼ cups margarine, lard, shortening, or butter (mix and match, whatever's on hand)

1. Mix and stir in a big bowl with an old wooden spoon, using much effort!
2. Spoon drop onto greased or floured cookie sheets, and bake at 375° till brown around edges, 10-12 minutes.

My mother was 43 years old when I, her ninth and last child, was born. She was a heavy-set woman with a strong build and lots of energy. Providing for nine children on a seventy-five-acre farm was no small challenge and especially so during the Depression years. Frugality, family cooperation, and lots of hard work is why we never went hungry those years.

Besides cooking, sewing, and managing the chores for the household, my mother's roles included gardening, harvesting, and preserving vegetables plus fruit from trees and berry patches. This included raising our own potatoes for the whole year. It was very important to Mother to raise and preserve enough food for her family to last until the next harvest.

It was also important to her to take advantage of all the products produced on the farm. She assisted my dad in the processing of maple sugar water to make maple syrup each spring. My father would butcher beef and pork, and Mother would preserve this meat together with her chickens used for this purpose. With cream from our unsold weekend milk supply, she would ask me to churn the cream to make butter. She would use the buttermilk obtained from making the butter, cottage cheese, and cheese to make pancakes or to bake with. Seldom did she throw anything usable away.

Mother also took advantage of the grains my father harvested. I can still see the big iron pot full of whole grain wheat cooking on her wood-burning iron cookstove. It would be enough for several breakfast meals. Another time the iron pot would be full of cornmeal mush, which we ate with milk and sugar for the evening meal. The rest would be poured in a shallow pan to harden overnight for fried mush in the morning. This would then be served with tomato gravy. Another time the pot would hold whole corn kernels for hominy which was a specialty for the family.

Every Sunday morning, there was a pot of rice cooking on the stove that she served with milk, sugar, and sometimes raisins, which we all loved. This was usually the only time we got to have rice since potatoes were much more economical for us.

From little up, my daily jobs were always to make sure there was plenty of wood in the wood chest for Mother's cookstove and to set the table three times daily for the family meals. Mother did most of the meal planning and cooking, but she involved me for the most mundane jobs and errands, like going to the basement to get potatoes and/or canned foods for her.

Mother raised chickens for both laying hens and for the meat. My role was assisting Mother with the butchering and dressing of the chickens, which was not my favorite job. She had me holding the chickens' legs while she did her job.

She processed chickens, not only for eating and canning, but also to sell to her customers in town. She frequently asked me to accompany her as she drove to town on her horse-drawn vehicle, which usually took us an hour. She would then have me hold the horse's reins as she delivered her products from door to door. This was also a social time for Mother as she loved to visit with clients. I did not enjoy waiting for Mother because it would get long and boring. In spite of this, it was a privilege to accompany her. Sometimes she would reward me with a ten-cent ice cream cone. It also meant a break from the farm work. ❧ *Elena Yoder*

❧

Mama always wore an apron over her homemade house dresses. I remember Wednesdays after school, we made homemade noodles and thin squares for pot pie. My job was to hang the long strands over linen towels across the backs of our wooden kitchen chairs. After they were dry, the noodles went into paper bags. We made noodles every week. Sometimes I was sent next door to take noodles to a neighbor who lived alone. Mama taught me to share.

Every summer Mama, my sister, baby brother, and I went to the cottage, which was in the mountains. Daddy came up after work. Mama had her own things there. She had a collection of plates from the Jewel Tea Company.

The rest of the year we lived with my grandma—Mama said she was glad to keep house for her as the Depression made it too difficult to go housekeeping with Daddy. Her happiest times were playing with us and sewing our clothes for school. She didn't need a pattern. We showed her a dress in the Sears Catalog, and she could copy it without a pattern.

❧ *Jean Harris Robinson*

Table Talk

Betty Pellman with daughter, Phyllis, age 3, in a photo taken as a Father's Day gift for Richard Pellman, Phyllis' dad.

There was nothing like "I don't want any," or "I don't like that" at our table. We ate whatever we were served. I don't remember any battles because we knew the outcome before we started.

But there was one thing I couldn't bear. Milk. I really hated it. So I just let my glass sit on the table. This was a little hard on my dad, who worked for Turkey Hill Dairy, and we lived on one of the Dairy farms in those days.

Ma bought really nifty cups to put my milk in. She got crazy straws. I was not persuaded.

Finally, she cut funny pictures out of magazines and pasted them face-up on the bottoms of my glasses of milk.

She knew I was a nosy kid. And she had figured out how to get in front of me on my milk protest. I drained my glass from there on without a whimper.　　　*Phyllis Pellman Good*

❧

When I was very young, say 4 or 5, my mom made me and my little brother a snack of soda crackers and mayonnaise. She told us that this was a very special snack, and it was something grownups ate. She let us eat it in the front room on the coffee table while we watched some TV. We were in hog heaven!

Decades later, Mom told me that there were a few times that we did not always have food in the house because of budgeting snafus or because she did not have the chance to get to the grocery store. We were a one-car family, and Dad had it for work everyday. She had hungry kids and she was always a clever person, so she did her best to make sure we were content.　　　*Jill Adams*

❧

When we were old enough to sit in the high chair, we were required to be at the breakfast table. We ate all meals together and after dinner, a great highlight of the day was taking turns to bring in the mail.

One routine that we kept was to dust mop the kitchen after each meal. What a time saver to get the crumbs before they were spread around!　　　*Mary B. Sensenig*

Mary Sensenig's mother, Edwina R. Weaver with some "grands" in 1989.

Mealtime is about the happiest remembrance of my childhood even though my memories might be embellished a tad.

Setting the table fell to my sister and me. Ice in glasses, bread and butter, and a few hot pads on the table were part of the routine. When our dad arrived home, we'd clamor to the table—five kids seven years apart—to enjoy a hot casserole and canned vegetables heated and ready in a serving dish. We were very hearty eaters, by the way!

Stuffed shells, lasagna, chicken and rice dishes, and home-made tuna casserole made many appearances. A particularly amazing meal was Mom's Italian meatloaf (meatloaves in our case), oven-baked potatoes, and peas. I used her recipe for years.

My family sat down together to eat. We were all home, in those days of the '70s. The few activities that some of my brothers were involved in didn't seem to interfere with the majority of our evenings. Belly laughing, a bit of tattling, and reviewing the school day were the norm. Dishes fell to two very sad children afterward with Dad doing an inspection before we were excused.

I make every effort I can to have a good dinner for my boys and husband these days, not necessarily something costly, but I desire to show some thought. I want my family to be glad to be home—like I was!   *Jodi*

<hr />

My dear mom nurtured our family with many delicious meals. My father worked nights, so we always ate dinner right after my sister and I returned home from school since Dad left for work at 4 p.m. sharp. My parents strongly believed sharing a family meal together was an important family tradition.

My father was Italian and actually taught my mom how to cook. We had a *lot* of pasta: spaghetti and lentils, cabbage and mostaccioli, orzo and peas, beans and ditallini (otherwise known as pasta fazool), and of course the traditional marinara sauce with meatballs or braciole that simmered on the stove all day.

We always had fruit for dessert during the week, but on weekends, Mom would bake her delicious

Rose C. Speicher eating spinach in 1958. Her dad's note on back of the photo reads: "Boy! Oh boy! Did you love <u>spinach</u>, you just couldn't get it in your mouth fast enough!"

lemon meringue and coconut creme pies and homemade banana bread.

Since Dad's family owned a produce company, we ate a lot of vegetables. When most other kids in the neighborhood were eating canned corn and green beans, we were eating everything from fresh broccoli and kale to cardoon and dandelion greens. We would also drink the water the dandelion greens were cooked in—a warm, earthy, soothing broth. It's still one of my favorite comfort foods.

There was a food ritual I especially looked forward to on Christmas day: the Peeling of the Pomegranate. My dad was the patriarch in the family. He would gather all the young cousins around a table and then proceed to slowly and methodically peel a plump, ripe, and juicy pomegranate. I remember laughing hysterically with my cousins as the bright red juice squirted all over. We all wanted to touch the intriguing, white waxy membrane that surrounded the seeds. It seemed time stood still as we anxiously and attentively waited for the first taste of the succulent seeds that my dad would carefully divide between all of us. Eating that pomegranate was a pure sensual delight, but it was more than just a sweet treat—it was a symbol of love between generations.

Rose C. Speicher

❧

Mama started getting supper ready well before time to eat. Supper was always a full meal with meat, salad, vegetables, bread, and dessert. Mama had supper on the table at 6 p.m., timed to be ready by the time Daddy got home and had changed out of his suit.

My sister and I had to set the table beforehand. This nightly routine included moving the table out from the wall, putting up the dropleaf, and putting on the table pads and the table cloth. Then we put on the plates, silverware, napkins, salt and pepper, and butter. Then all the food was placed on the table, with the meat always in front of Daddy. We never ate until after the blessing was said.

The four of us sat down together at this big long table with my sister next to me on the long side and Mama and Daddy at each end. The TV was on the opposite side of the room. Sometimes the TV was on to hear important things happening in the news, but usually we learned "pleasant conversation" that was appropriate for the dinner table. The food was always abundant: lettuce and tomato salad, bowls of hot fried potatoes, peas, steak, gravy, and unsweetened iced tea. We ate and had seconds and sometimes thirds, and then dessert came. To think that we ate like that every day! It was wonderful.

We were always expected to use correct table manners: left hand in your lap, chew with your mouth closed, don't talk with food in your mouth. I remember learning to pass the food. Since my sister and I were in the middle we were the "passers" between Mama and Daddy. With any complaint on our part, we were told that passing food builds character.

After dinner, every thing went in reverse. All was removed from the table, the leaf was put down, and the table was put back against the wall. The table cloth was shaken out on the back porch, and the dishes were washed by my mother, and either my sister or I dried the dishes.

That dinner table is still in the family. Our married daughter has it now, after I used it for a few years. It really isn't as big in real life as it is in my memories. But it played a big part in our family life—it is where my sister and I learned to be civilized.   ❧ *Diane Blaising*

When we visited Grandma, Mom and Grandma would talk together for days on end. I always wanted to be a part of their "big girl" talk.

Grandma would make hot tea, and I was allowed to drink a cup with them and add a sugar cube or two. I felt so grown up without my sisters around—just me, my mom, and my grandma. As soon as my tea was gone or I tired of it, I was shooed out of the kitchen, and they could talk without my ears around. *Lisa Harder*

The medicine cup of M&M's that Shelly Burns' mother used to teach table manners.

A fond memory I have of meals around the table was when we were learning manners in school. Mom would give each one of us children a medicine cup full of M&M's. During the meal, if we caught someone chewing with their mouth open, putting their elbows on the table, etc., they had to give us one of their M&M's. After the meal was finished, we got to eat all the M&M's in our medicine cups, some of us purposing to mind our manners better next time! *Shelley Burns*

My parents were raised during the Depression, and there was no such thing as not eating what was in front of you. My dad taught us that if someone made you food, you were gracious and ate no matter what you thought, and you thanked them for fixing you food.

The lesson became very clear when we visited my great-aunt in Minnesota. She figured my dad, being a Southerner, would love fried chicken. Actually, he hated chicken, so Mom did not serve it at home. My dad ate the beautiful dinner with a smile with three fascinated children watching and graciously thanked my great-aunt for fixing such a beautiful meal for us. She was tickled with his compliment and never knew what he really thought about chicken. We never griped about the food in front of us again.   *Thea Schroeder*

꽃

My mom spent most of her time in the kitchen, but it wasn't just cooking. My dad watched a lot of sports on the television, and that bored my mother and me, so we would sit at the kitchen table for hours playing card games. I swear that's how I became good at math—from keeping score. Now when I go home to visit, Mom and I still sit at the table and play card games.   *Kelly Chiemingo*

꽃

Sometimes Mom cooked or we kids cooked if Mom was helping milk the cows with Dad. Other times Dad cooked. Dad made Spanish rice once. It was very adventurous of him. We liked the recipe, and it became his signature dish.

We all ate together—often late at night at 7:30 or sometimes 9:00 in the summer. There was much work to do on the farm. We talked about the farm mostly, the latest gossip, church news, and family events.   *Regina Martin*

꽃

At our house, we children knew that we had to eat a serving of each main dish whether we liked it or not. After learning that our cousins didn't have to eat food they didn't like, we started to complain about the dishes we didn't enjoy. If Mom cooked a dish that we didn't like, we let her know!

Mother told us how impolite it was to criticize and that from now on, we weren't allowed to talk like that at the table. However, since Mom didn't list a penalty for disobeying this rule, we disregarded it. My mother was at her wits' end as to how to deal with this ingratitude.

Then she came up with a brilliant idea. To this day, I can't remember which of the older two children made the offensive comment about hating peas. My mother looked that child and promptly gave him another serving of peas. She told us that from then on whenever we complained about a dish, we would get another serving of it. Bad habits take a while to break, and it took several weeks until we remembered to not complain about the food she made! ❧ *Anita Troyer*

❧

My mother almost always cooked, although my sister and I helped. I loved when we had Dagwoods—big sandwiches with anything you wanted. My favorite treat was banana splits. Every year when Peter Pan would air on TV, we would get to watch TV while we ate. We would have chili with crackers and cheese and pickles. ❧ *Rhonda*

❧

Mom always cooked, because Dad never came home from work before 7:00 at night. We all sat down for supper nightly, with meat or fish or chicken, potatoes or rice, and always fresh vegetables. Mom's cooking was so good that neighbors always seemed to be dropping by just about suppertime.

That was the time when we all discussed our days and shared highs and lows. There was no TV in the dining room—in fact, there was no TV in the house until I was 11. We were all the entertainment each other needed, and there was never a dull moment. ❧ *Jeff Thal*

Mom was always the cook. Dad would seldom go out to eat because, in his words, he married the best cook in the world, and why should he eat somewhere else. McDonald's only served to irritate him so much that no one else could enjoy their meals!

Often times my dad and brothers would "invent" things during a meal. One time in particular they figured out how to load that newfangled hifi system with records by rigging up some kind of suspension system along the sides of the living room that could drop records one at a time onto the turntable without anyone having to get up to do it. A lot of laughter is what I recall. ❧ *Ginny Walls*

I remember an event that took place after my first semester at Goshen College, when I was home for Christmas holiday. On the last Sunday evening before my return to college, we were all seated at the kitchen table, including Clarence, age 13, Babs, 9, and Johnny, 4. Little Johnny just sat across from me at the table silently, not eating, playing with his food. Ever the big sister, I told Mother that she should enforce proper eating habits with him. Johnny dropped his fork, lowered his head, glowered at me, and said in a low voice, "I'll be glad when *you're* gone!"

It was important to Mother that each part of the meal be done properly with attention and love. She even bought special jelly jars with an embossed design on the bottom, so that when the jelly was inverted into its glass serving dish, a pretty star or flower appeared. At the end of a growing season, Mother would have a good 200 or more jellies and jams from a wide variety of fruits in her cupboard ready to give as gifts or serve at the table.

We had several fruit trees in our yard, but no space for a vegetable garden, and no need of one. Mother's parents on the farm kept us supplied with seasonal vegetables, and Mother went downtown to Lancaster's famous market twice a week by trolley, her market basket on her arm. I still have that basket. She had her favorite vendors for fresh bread, eggs, home-made noodles, freshly ground horseradish, meat, and a chat.   ❧ *Naomi Brubaker Fast*

❧

I was an only child and was included in just about every-thing that went on in our family. I learned to enjoy most of the foods my parents ate, and my mother and I often cooked together.

I especially enjoyed going to market with her. Fridays we would go to Green Dragon Farmer's Market in Ephrata, PA, for our meat and fresh produce. Friday evenings we "ate supper out of the market basket." We'd have fresh lunch meat and cheeses on fresh rolls and homemade potato chips. Sticky buns were also a great treat. My parents liked cup cheese, a market favorite, but I refused to eat that smelly cheese.

We lived in a double house with my grandparents, and the walls were rather thin. Our kitchen tables were located at the same spots next to the dividing wall. If we knocked on the wall and spoke loudly, we could talk to one another. Sometimes we even sent an invitation—via a knock and a shout—to join us for dinner or dessert! ✿ *Susan J. Heil*

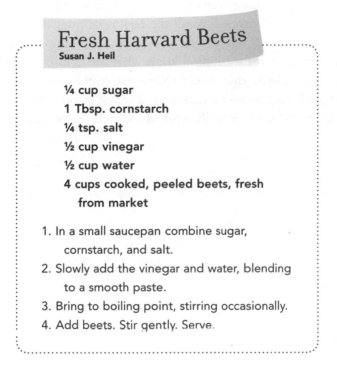

Fresh Harvard Beets
Susan J. Heil

¼ cup sugar

1 Tbsp. cornstarch

¼ tsp. salt

½ cup vinegar

½ cup water

4 cups cooked, peeled beets, fresh
  from market

1. In a small saucepan combine sugar, cornstarch, and salt.
2. Slowly add the vinegar and water, blending to a smooth paste.
3. Bring to boiling point, stirring occasionally.
4. Add beets. Stir gently. Serve.

Mealtime in our home was social time! Daddy and Mother worked very hard to have everyone at the table before we held hands, bowed our heads, and had prayer. We often sang in four-part harmony God is Good to the tune of Take My Life and Let it Be. We loved to sing around the table, blending our voices, being one with each other and at peace. Once the amen was said, we instantly started talking, carrying on two or three conversations at once until Daddy or Mother would say, "One at a time!"

I clearly remember stalling over kidney beans, pintos, garbanzos, white beans, split peas, and lentils. I hated them with a passion! As a young girl, it seemed to me that Mother was always making beans, and an eight-quart kettle could last several days. I can still recall the feeling of utter dread that washed over my heart when I'd hear Mother dumping beans into the sink for washing. I knew what was coming and the loss of appetite that would follow me to the table. Several times I tried to invite myself to a friend's house to escape supper, but it never really worked too well.   ❧ *Sara Meyers*

Special Meals

I will never forget my seventh birthday. Mom made a beautiful cake she called a sunshine cake. It was three layers with a wonderful custard between the layers. She frosted it with a beautiful fluffy frosting she had tinted a soft yellow. She left a white square in the middle and spelled my name in gold and silver dragees. She also put real fresh violets on it. I still think it was one of the most beautiful cakes I have ever seen. My uncle came and brought ice cream, the rarest of treats.

For the meal, Mom made Pennsylvania Dutch chicken pot pie. She knew that was my favorite thing to eat. She also made crusty rolls to wipe up every last drop of gravy and had fresh sliced tomatoes on the side. I will never forget that day. What really made it special was that I had been in the hospital for several months with pernicious anemia. I only weighed 27 pounds, I have been told. After being forced to eat liver every single day and even finding it ground up and hiding in my desserts, you can understand how overjoyed I was to eat my mom's wonderful food and to be home again.

❧ *Helene M. Stafford*

❧

The day after I had my wisdom teeth cut out, we had company for dinner, and Mom fixed roast beef, mashed potatoes, and gravy. The smell was heavenly, but there was no way at all I could eat it. I was having a terrible time, miserably laying in bed. I guess Mom felt sorry for me, because she ran the roast beef and mashed potatoes through the food processor and brought it to me. Not pretty to look at, but the flavor was amazing!

❧ *Susan*

❧

We didn't have much growing up. One day prior to payday, my mother realized she had very little in her pocket and three kids to feed. She came home with a loaf of bread and a dozen eggs and informed us that we would be eating Special Eggs for dinner. Special Eggs were just eggs in a hole (eggs fried in cut-out bread slices), but to us kids, it was the most clever, exciting dinner we ever had. We are now 41, 37, and 35, and we still call them Special Eggs.

❧ *Kathleen Brawley*

E very year she let me pick out a cake design for my birthday. One year I picked what was actually a fiftieth wedding anniversary cake with gold mini-roses cascading down from the top. *Doug Poole*

I worked one and a half hours from home when I was a teenager, and I'd arrive home on the weekends hungry for Mom's bland, simple cooking. I loved "Amish noodles" cooked in rich chicken broth layered with mashed potatoes and gravy all in one pile on our plates. I think that Mom learned that delicious combination through her Amish ancestry because my aunts and cousins still serve meals like that. A good ending to the meal was plain Jello and oatmeal cake with broiled coconut topping.

Another special meal she made was a vegetable stew served with warm vanilla cornstarch pudding (we just called it cornstarch) on the side. Even after fifty-plus years, cornstarch is the go-along with stew for me! *Marlene Graber*

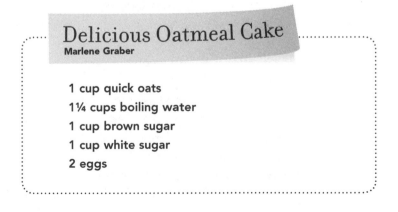

Delicious Oatmeal Cake
Marlene Graber

1 cup quick oats
1¼ cups boiling water
1 cup brown sugar
1 cup white sugar
2 eggs

½ cup (1 stick) butter or margarine
1⅓ cups flour
1 tsp. baking soda
1 tsp. vanilla
1 tsp. salt
1 tsp. cinnamon

Topping:
6 Tbsp. melted butter
4 Tbsp. cream or milk
1 cup brown sugar
1 cup coconut
½ cup chopped nuts
½ tsp. vanilla

1. Soak oatmeal in the boiling water. Set aside until cool.
2. Cream butter, eggs and sugars. Mix in other ingredients, including oatmeal, and pour in greased 9 x 13 pan.
3. Bake at 350° for 35 minutes.
4. While baking, mix topping. Spread on baked cake while warm, and broil until topping starts to bubble and brown.

❦

The gray days of midwinter in Wisconsin were a bleak time. To cheer us up, my mother and grandmother made up a holiday—the SuperCelebration of Holidays—that included elements of all the holidays. Each person chose to celebrate his or her favorite holiday with dress, some entertainment, and, of course, the food. Decorations were a total mish-mash of holiday decorations in a wild riot of color. And the feasting! Christmas sweet rolls, Easter ham loaf, whipped potatoes with parsnips, pies, cakes, and corned beef and sausages, and, well, the celebration meal was a belly filler.

As I have aged and gained perspective, I now know that it was the love that flowed and surrounded each family member that gave such delight and memories. That love still colors my life! ❧ *Carol Parkey*

❧

When I was turning 16, my step-mom, Sandy, asked me what I wanted for my birthday meal. Boy, was I surprised! The thought of deciding what to have for dinner was exciting. I actually don't remember what I chose, because the thing that stands out to me was how special she made me feel. That event impacted me so much that when I started having my own children, I implemented the tradition into my own family.

My biological daughter got this special treat every year, and though it was special, she was used to it. But when we adopted our boys from Russia and they got the opportunity to choose their special birthday meals, I could see their eyes light up and hear the excitement in their voices.

This December will be their eighth birthday to spend with us, and each year they seem to start planning earlier and talking about what they will have. It is a *big* deal to them, and it warms my heart to be able to give them such a treat, just as it was a treat for me so many years before.

❧ *Nora Hofmans*

❧

The meal that I remember more than any other was the one my mother cooked the evening before she passed away in a car accident.

My aunt married a man of Mexican-Chinese ancestry, and they cooked a lot of authentic Mexican dishes. She taught my mom how to make several of them, but one of our favorite meals was fried tacos, Spanish rice, and refried beans.

I remember helping my mom prepare the tacos for frying that evening; little did I know that that would be the last meal I would ever help my mom prepare. The following morning, she was killed in a car wreck that we had on our way to school. I have never forgotten what she cooked that night so many years ago.   *LaRisa Morace*

❦

My brother, Ed, joined the Air Force after high school. Mom did not show any fear or sadness about Ed joining up and going away.

His girlfriend's parents were hosting a big going away party for him, and Mom was making potato salad for about twenty people. One of the serving bowls was a cut-glass bowl that had been her mother's, and just as she was finishing the salad, the cut-glass bowl dropped and broke with the salad in it. Glass shards and potato salad were everywhere, and Mom fell to her knees sobbing.

Normally she would rather choke than swear, but that afternoon I heard Mom say words that made me blush. Once she could stand up again, we quietly cleaned up the kitchen. I don't remember what she took in place of the salad, but she held her head high at the party.   *Carol Scott*

E very year my mom asked me what I wanted to eat on my birthday, and I always wanted her to make spaghetti. I always asked to help make it, but her reply was, "Maybe next year when you get a little older."

Finally, when I was about 9, she said I could help. She assembled all of the ingredients. As she chopped away, she called out the herbs for me to put in. I forgot which ones I had put in, but I did my best.

Then came the time to bake the cake. I asked her if we could make one with a little doll in the middle of the cake that became her dress. She sent me to my room to bring one of my small dolls. After several minutes of washing her, my mom put the doll in the middle of the cake batter and popped it in the oven. When she took it out of the oven, the doll had melted. I was in tears because my doll had been killed.

Then, to make things worse, we sat down to eat the spaghetti, and it was too salty to eat. My mom dried my tears and said, "Baby, we both have made mistakes today that we have learned from. Now go clean up, and we'll go out to eat and get you a new baby doll." *Linda Wade*

ૐ

M y twelfth birthday meal was exotic. Mom made a huge bear steak for me that she got from a local hunter. It was the last time I ate bear. *Teri McHugh*

ૐ

W hen I graduated from high school, my mom threw me a huge party. She made macaroni tuna salad, potato salad, turkey loaf, and ham loaf with corn and green beans on the side and her famous homemade buns.

She ordered a special graduation cake too. There was tons of food and many, many guests. She was so proud of me, and she made sure that everyone knew it. ❧ *Bonnie Pruett*

Macaroni Tuna Salad
Bonnie Pruett

3 cups elbow macaroni cooked, drained and
   cooled
15-oz. can sweet green peas, drained
1 medium onion, diced
5 eggs hard-boiled, peeled, and chopped
1 cup Miracle Whip salad dressing
Mrs. Dash Seasoning, to taste

1. In large bowl, mix all ingredients until well blended.
   If the salad seems a little dry, add more Miracle
   Whip until it is moist enough to suit you.
2. Chill 2-3 hours before serving.

Potato Salad
Bonnie Pruett

5 lbs. potatoes
6 eggs, hardboiled, chopped (may hold back 1-2
   to slice for garnish)
1 large onion chopped
1-2 cups Miracle Whip salad dressing
3 Tbsp regular yellow mustard, or spicy mustard
   if desired
2-3 tsp. sugar

1. Boil the potatoes whole, in their skins, until done but still firm. Set aside to cool.
2. When cool, peel and cut potatoes into bite-sized pieces. Put into a large bowl, add chopped onion and eggs, and mix well.
3. In small bowl, combine salad dressing and mustard. Mix well. Add sugar and mix again.
4. Pour mixture over potato mixture in large bowl. Mix gently. Place sliced eggs on top to decorate if you wish.
5. Chill 2-3 hours before serving.

※

When I was 13, my dad was hurt in a mine cave-in in December. My dad cried for the first time I remember. He felt like he had let us down because he could not work for several months while his leg healed. My mom assured him all would be well. We didn't have much to begin with, so we kids thought our Christmas dinner would be potato sandwiches.

Away from Dad's bed, Mom called me and my brother to come help her. We went up in the attic and helped her bring down little Christmas presents. She had bought small things (they weren't toys) during the summer. Then she showed us cookies she baked in little batches while we were at school. She went next door to our neighbor's to retrieve the turkey she had bought from the butcher on a monthly installment payment plan.

When Dad saw everything on Christmas, he cried again. Seeing my little sister's face that Christmas morning will live in my heart and mind forever because she was only 5 and so excited that Santa didn't forget where we lived. My dad was happiest of all and kept praising Mom's management and ingenuity.

❧ Helen Arano

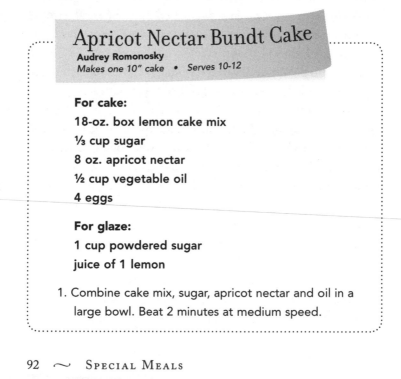

My mom loved to throw dinner parties for her friends, and they played cards after dinner. Rock Cornish hens were always the main course, and she always made a bundt cake for dessert.

When I moved out on my own many years ago, she gave me the cake recipe. I have followed my mom's tradition by serving it at my own dinner parties as well as at bridal showers, baby showers, and bunco parties. Several of my friends have requested the recipe, which honors my mom who passed away in 2010.

❧ Audrey Romonosky

Apricot Nectar Bundt Cake
Audrey Romonosky
Makes one 10" cake • Serves 10-12

For cake:
18-oz. box lemon cake mix
⅓ cup sugar
8 oz. apricot nectar
½ cup vegetable oil
4 eggs

For glaze:
1 cup powdered sugar
juice of 1 lemon

1. Combine cake mix, sugar, apricot nectar and oil in a large bowl. Beat 2 minutes at medium speed.

2. Add eggs, one at a time, beating after each.

3. Pour into a greased and floured bundt pan. Bake at 325° for 1 hour or until cake springs back when lightly touched and cake tester comes out clean when testing for doneness.

4. Cool on rack right side up in pan for 15 minutes. Remove cake from pan to finish cooling.

5. To glaze, blend powdered sugar with lemon juice. Pour over top and sides of warm cake.

Several years ago my wife Shirley was very sick and spent spent weeks in the hospital and a rehab center. My mom knew that I worried about Shirley and that I had made arrangements with work for half days. So as to relieve my worries, Mom would stay with Shirley from 8 am until I got there. If she could not be there, she made sure a family friend was there. Still Mom worried about me not eating right or taking care of myself.

For my birthday, mom cleared it with the rehab center to throw a surprise party. When I showed up at the rehab center on my birthday in September, Shirley was not in her room, and I was told that she was in the dining room visiting. When I got to the dining room, the whole family was there for a surprise birthday meal. Mom had made my favorite meal—a huge Thanksgiving dinner. Not only was this a celebration of my life but a celebration of hope for those in the rehab center.

Frank Hemenway

One beautiful summer afternoon in late June, my mom was planning my first-ever birthday party when I was 6. She asked me what I would like to have for lunch at the party. I said, "Watermelon seed soup and watermelon." Actually it was an Italian beef shank soup with orzo pasta, which my sister and I called watermelon seeds since they were the same shape.

I also requested brown cows—a glass of root beer with a dip of vanilla ice cream in it. I loved to watch the root beer get foamy when Mom added the ice cream.

Rose C. Speicher, age 20 months, in 1958. This table is where Rose and her friends ate "watermelon-seed soup" a few years later. Note on back of photo: "Daddy & Mommie bought you this pretty little yellow table and chairs for your very own, on Xmas 1957. Please smile for us always."

It was probably the only party my friends ever attended where they were served beef shank soup, watermelon, and brown cows, but they loved it!   ❧ *Rose C. Speicher*

Beef Shank Soup
Rose C. Speicher

16 cups water
3-4 beef shanks, rinsed and trimmed of excess fat
5 large carrots peeled and kept whole
1 white onion peeled and kept whole
4 ribs celery, cut in half, celery leaves
    included if available
5 tsp. beef base or 5 beef bouillon
    cubes
handful fresh parsley, chopped
14½-oz. can original or Italian stewed
    tomatoes
¾ cup uncooked orzo
grated Pecorino Romano or Parmesan,
    as desired
black pepper, to taste

1. Fill 8-quart stockpot with the water.
2. Add carrots, celery onion and beef
   shank.
3. Bring to a boil. Add beef base and
   parsley.
4. Simmer about 2-3 hours until meat is
   tender, skimming off foam as it rises to
   the top.
5. Remove meat and discard bones but
   reserve the marrow from inside the
   bones in a large bowl.
6. Shred meat into bite-size pieces. This should be
   easy since meat will be fall-apart tender.
7. Remove all veggies and put in large bowl with
   marrow.

This is the best comfort soup ever—my husband says it's his all-time favorite soup! I ate bowls of it growing up and so did our children.

Pureeing veggies and adding them back into the soup is also a great way to get young kids to eat their veggies without a fuss.

❧

When I was 9 years of age, I had appendicitis. Complications occurred, and I was in the hospital for a very long time. While I was in the hospital, I refused to eat their food. I lived on Butterscotch Tastykakes, which Mom brought every day to the hospital. When I returned home, Mom made stuffed chicken. She was scared for me at the dinner table. She told me I ate so much at dinner that night that she thought I was going to burst my stitches. I guess I really missed her cooking. ❧ *Connie Sloan*

❧

My brothers and I decided to make our mother breakfast in bed. I was 7, and they were 9 and 10. My 9-year-old brother dropped eggs on the carpet and was trying to scrub it. I was in charge of the coffee. I filled the percolator with water, plugged it in, added three scoops of coffee, and put the lid on.

My 10-year-old brother was starting bacon, and he told me to go ahead and mix up the pancakes. I had seen Mother mix cakes, so instead of using a wooden spoon in the bowl, I plugged in the electric mixer and turned it on high, which caused most of the ingredients to fly out of the bowl, to my dismay. Due to the noise of the beaters hitting the side of the bowl, Mother woke up.

There we were—eggs stuck in the carpet, flour everywhere, and bacon sizzling. She never yelled, just asked us if we needed help and proceeded to the coffee pot with her favorite cup. She took one sip and dropped her cup—it was thick with grounds. I remember afterwards feeling sad that it was my fault her favorite cup was broken, but she comforted me and said it was okay, that I had done my best. Years later, I found a similar cup and gave it to her for Christmas.

Tracy Orr

❧

We always had a Valentine's supper with the whole family. Everything was heart-shaped that could possibly be cut, carved, or molded into hearts. We had meatloaf, sometimes shaped into a big heart, sometimes into small individual ones. Scalloped potatoes were made with sliced potatoes carved into hearts on the top of the pan. The lettuce salad had hearts of meat and cheese, and the bread was cut into hearts with a cookie cutter.

We ate by candlelight until the boys fussed they would like to be able to see what they're eating. We've gotten together for a Valentine's supper several times since most of us married, and the boys don't fuss about the candlelight anymore—unless it's for tradition's sake. *Jan Byler*

O ne of my siblings' and my favorite events at our house was fondue night. Mom would prepare two types of fondue. One was a rich, delicious cheese fondue with things like fresh bread, broccoli, and cauliflower to dip in the cheese. The other was a chocolate dessert fondue with fresh fruit, marshmallows, and pound cake for dipping.

The whole meal was an event, complete with sparkling cider and candlelight. We'd sit at that table for well over an hour talking about anything and everything, laughing at my younger brother's antics, and slowly but surely making our way through that pot of rich fondue.

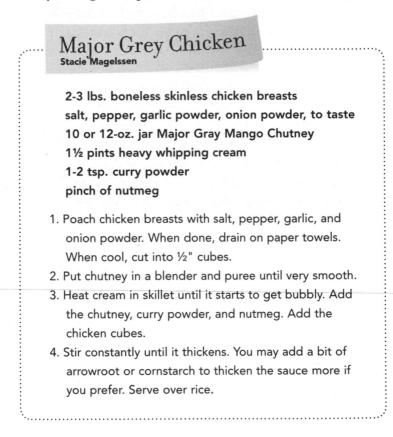

Major Grey Chicken
Stacie Magelssen

2-3 lbs. boneless skinless chicken breasts
salt, pepper, garlic powder, onion powder, to taste
10 or 12-oz. jar Major Gray Mango Chutney
1½ pints heavy whipping cream
1-2 tsp. curry powder
pinch of nutmeg

1. Poach chicken breasts with salt, pepper, garlic, and onion powder. When done, drain on paper towels. When cool, cut into ½" cubes.
2. Put chutney in a blender and puree until very smooth.
3. Heat cream in skillet until it starts to get bubbly. Add the chutney, curry powder, and nutmeg. Add the chicken cubes.
4. Stir constantly until it thickens. You may add a bit of arrowroot or cornstarch to thicken the sauce more if you prefer. Serve over rice.

This was long before any of the fondue restaurants that have become so popular, and none of my other friends had even heard of fondue. I remember feeling so proud that my mom knew how to make something so decadent and special. Fondue night was Mom's unspoken way of telling us how much she loved us. I've carried on the tradition with my own family.

My mom made so many incredible meals and desserts in the kitchen that it's hard to narrow them down to my favorite, but if I had to pick, I'd say it's her Major Gray Chicken recipe. It's what I begged her to make every year on my birthday.

❧ *Stacie Magelssen*

❧

I treasure the memory of a special meal that Mom made for my thirteenth birthday. She invited my cousins and friends for an all-out tea party. She decorated and cooked and baked until she was weary—barely getting any sleep the night before the party. It was all so that I could have a special entrance into the teen years. I remember that she even made a cake that was shaped like a teapot. I was a gangly, pimply, emotional adolescent, but to her, I was a princess.

❧ *MarJanita Geigley*

❧

One tribute to my mother's hospitality came from an unusual source. One afternoon during the 1940s, she received a call from Dad at work: would she accept a guest at the table that evening? Naturally she had a nice meal ready for her unknown visitor, who turned out to be none other than the Lone Ranger himself.

Dad was designing a toy modeled after this famous cowboy hero, who was in town to endorse the product. Dad bowed his head to bless the food, during which the Ranger removed his trademark black mask. We enjoyed a delicious meal together. Afterward the Ranger told Dad that this was the only time he had ever taken off his mask in public. That's how powerful my mother's hospitality was.

Naomi Brubaker Fast

The day before I turned 8, my father had a paralyzing stroke. We were at the dinner table, talking as usual, when he stiffened suddenly and fell to the floor. The paramedics came, and he was rushed to the hospital in an ambulance.

It was chaotic and frightening. But I have no memory of it, even though I was sitting right next to Dad. I don't remember Dad being in the hospital for weeks or his recovery at home. I guess I blocked it all out.

What I *do* remember is my mother making me a homemade mandarin orange cake with orange zest frosting, blowing up balloons, hanging streamers, and overseeing ten 8-year-old girls shrieking and running wild. In all the pictures, she appears calm and smiling.

My mother must have been overwhelmed with concern for my father and longing to be with him in the hospital, but she made a point of making my birthday special and carrying on for my sake when her own world was falling apart. It took over a year, but eventually Dad made a full recovery.

Donika Engstrom

I remember the first time we had my special homemade birthday cake called Nothing Cake. When my sister was asked if she wanted a slice of Nothing Cake, she thought it was a joke and said she didn't want any. Boy, was she surprised when the rest of us were served cake and ice cream, and she only got ice cream! It is still my favorite cake.

❧ Becky McClees

Nothing Cake
Becky McClees

½ cup (1 stick) butter
1½ cups sugar
2 eggs
2½ cups flour
2 tsp. baking soda
20-oz. can crushed pineapple with juice

Nothing Frosting:
1½ cups sugar
½ cup (1 stick) butter
1 cup evaporated milk
1½ cups flaked coconut
1 cup chopped pecans *or* walnuts

1. Cream butter and sugar. Beat in eggs one at a time.
2. Sift flour and soda. Add to creamed mixture alternately with crushed pineapple.
3. Pour into 9 x 13 greased, floured baking pan.
4. Bake at 350° for 30-35 minutes, or until tester inserted in middle comes out clean.
5. Make frosting in a sauce pan, heat sugar, butter, and milk. Bring to a boil and cook until thick, about 15 minutes, stirring to prevent scorching.
6. Remove from heat. Stir in coconut and nuts. Frost cake while frosting is warm.

❧

I remember one night my parents were going out, and we were allowed to stay home without a baby sitter. That was a big deal.

I think my mum felt guilty, so she asked us what we wanted for dinner. "Anything you want," she said. We picked fish sticks and banana pudding. She made us the biggest plate of fish sticks and added extra bananas into our pudding.

She kept saying, "Are you sure this is all you want?" As kids, we couldn't have been happier. It really made our evening—being allowed to eat just fish sticks and pudding for dinner. ❧ *Debby Lindsey*

❧

O ur favorite meals usually involved eating out because we didn't have much money, and eating out was a special occasion. Chinese food was our family favorite (I'm part Chinese.). My father would order all of our favorites, and we would share them.

My favorite birthday cake is a family recipe—Dobash Cake. ❧ *Deb Becker and Christen Chew*

Dobash Cake
Deb Becker and Christen Chew

16-oz. box devil's food cake mix

3 eggs

½ cup (1 stick) melted butter or margarine

1 Tbsp. oil

3-oz. box instant chocolate pudding

1 can 7-Up soda (1¼ cups)

Frosting:
1 cup Nestle Quik cocoa
2 cups cold water
4 Tbsp. cornstarch
3 Tbsp. margarine

1. Mix all ingredients together, leaving the 7-Up as the last ingredient to be added.
2. Pour into a greased 9 x 13 cake pan. Bake at 350° for 40 minutes or until the fork comes out clean.
3. Mix all dry frosting ingredients together in a saucepan, then gradually add the cold water, mixing until smooth.
4. Cook until it boils, then continue cooking until it becomes liquid enough to pour over the cake, but thick enough to pour evenly.
5. Allow to cool. Enjoy!

I remember being a teenager and not wanting to eat anything before school. My mom was so worried that I was so thin. She said she would fix me anything if I would just eat before I left for the day. Well, being a teenager, I loved those little frozen pizzas. My mom was at home and disabled at this time, and she would get up and make one little frozen pizza for me and sit with me while I ate it.

Kathy Ausburn

My husband and I were visiting from Chicago and staying with my husband's family. We got caught up longer than expected with his family who lived in the same town as my parents. We called my mom and dad and said we couldn't make it home for supper as planned and that they should go ahead and eat without us. She was so gracious.

I only found out by accident that she had gone to so much trouble for us, and we didn't show up. She had used a tablecloth that matched her special silverware and glasses. She had set the table with linen napkins and candles to adorn the feast. She was serving roast beef with all the trimmings.

Mom never said a word. I've cried more than a couple of tears over that event and want to grab back that opportunity to sit at her table.   ❧ *Ginny Walls*

❧

Thanksgiving Day of 1984 stands out in my memory as one of the most memorable times in the kitchen with my mom—as well as the saddest. My grandma, Mom's mom, died early that morning. I was pregnant with my first daughter, the first grandchild, and first great-grandchild— one that Grandma would never get to hold.

With heavy hearts and lots of tears, we made funeral arrangements, received phone calls from relatives, and made airline arrangements to get my brother home from the mountains of Colorado. We managed to make Thanksgiving dinner, reminiscing about Grandma. We even purposely burned the marshmallows on the sweet potatoes just like Grandma always did—although I don't think Grandma burned them on purpose. It just happened!

Since then, whoever makes the sweet potato casserole still burns the marshmallows in memory of Grandma.

Eight years later, Grandpa died on the exact same day. I

cooked Thanksgiving dinner for fifty-five people at my house the day after his funeral as all the relatives were still here. The skills in organization I learned from Mom in 1984 stayed with me, and I had dinner ready at noon for everyone and plenty of leftovers for supper that night. Mom taught me how to be organized in getting a big dinner on the table in spite of all the distractions.   *Sheila Kremer*

One year close to April Fool's Day, I found the perfect April Fool's Day meal in a magazine. Mom agreed to help me make it, and we invited a friend from church. We filled the clear glasses with red Jello since we usually served cranberry juice with ginger ale when company came over. We then made a "cake" out of meatloaf and "iced" it with mashed potatoes. Extra decorations on the cake were made with ketchup and mustard. There were some side dishes I don't recall.

Shelley Burns and her sister washing dishes.

The dessert was intended to look like a taco cup. We used waffle cups and put a scoop of chocolate ice cream in them. On top of this we placed green shredded coconut for lettuce, yellow shredded coconut for cheese, and candied cherries for tomatoes.

Not only was this meal fun to make, it was fun to eat and gave us something to laugh about that night.

    Shelley Burns

I n wintertime, I loved when Mom made tomato soup because she often poured it into two large soup mugs. I adored those mugs and grabbed every chance to use them. I felt so grown up sitting at the table, sipping my soup, and eating a toasted cheese sandwich on the side. To this day I think the best way to serve tomato soup is in a mug.

❧ *Bethanny Baumer*

A highlight of growing up was butchering day. We all looked forward to a wonderful supper of Dutch goose. Mom and I would scald, tug, and scrape the pig stomach to clean it to a snowy white.

She would prepare a dressing with sausage, bread, and potatoes moistened with eggs and milk. Then we would stuff the stomach, sew it shut, and slowly bake it to a nice golden brown. The aroma was heavenly. She served it with peas and applesauce. There was no need for dessert because we were all stuffed.

❧ *Phyllis Kauffman*

M y mom was one of eighteen children who grew up in a two-room home in southern Colorado. Mom was only educated to the eighth grade but was one of the smartest women you could ever know.

At Christmas, we would make cookies for weeks, and she would freeze them until needed—biscochitos, rum balls, pinwheels, Mexican wedding cookies, homemade fudge, brownies, divinity, and chocolate-covered pretzels.

When the day before Christmas came, we would be in the kitchen for twenty-four hours. We would prepare the turkey and ham and then make homemade cinnamon rolls and crescent rolls for the meal. Mom would make her cranberry relish, blueberry delight, mashed potatoes, sweet potatoes with pineapple and marshmallows, and a green salad.

All the dishes were prepared in Mom's best dishes—lots of carnival glass, which I have inherited now—and the table always looked so pretty. We would use the good china and set up a kids' table so everyone could eat together.

Henrietta Bastian

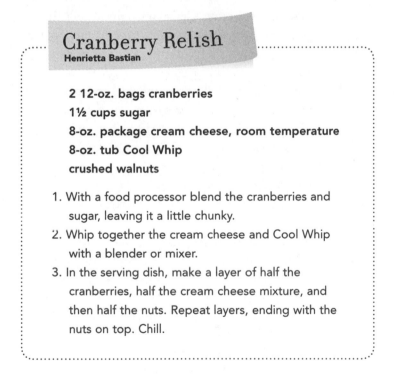

Cranberry Relish
Henrietta Bastian

2 12-oz. bags cranberries
1½ cups sugar
8-oz. package cream cheese, room temperature
8-oz. tub Cool Whip
crushed walnuts

1. With a food processor blend the cranberries and sugar, leaving it a little chunky.
2. Whip together the cream cheese and Cool Whip with a blender or mixer.
3. In the serving dish, make a layer of half the cranberries, half the cream cheese mixture, and then half the nuts. Repeat layers, ending with the nuts on top. Chill.

If I could return to one time in the kitchen with my
mother while I was growing up, it would be to the year
our family lived in a small apartment building with two other
American families in the picturesque German countryside.
Our apartment was quite spacious, yet the kitchen was tiny—
not much bigger than a child's play kitchen.

We laughed when we first spotted it and wondered how
we would cope for an entire year in that space. The tiny
freezer above the refrigerator barely had room for a few ice
cube trays. The refrigerator and pantry only had enough space
for a few days' groceries.

Well, we were up for a new adventure in a foreign country! We honed our beginning German language skills in the
town's grocery store, and I enjoyed my trips to the fragrant
bakery on the corner, its shelves resplendent with delicious
Bavarian pretzels, breads, and cakes.

My mother courageously shopped for groceries with
her limited understanding of German and the currency, my
newborn baby sister along for the ride in her stroller. We
always had to remember to shop for groceries for only a few
days at a time and to not overbuy groceries, like it is so easy
to do here in the United States.

I enjoyed planning meals with my mother, as we delib-
erately chose each dish and tried new spices and recipes. My
sister and I learned to carefully select our snacks after school,
rather than simply raiding the refrigerator as we did in the
United States. We had limited freezer space, so ice cream was
a special treat for our family.

We weren't able to visit our grandparents and family in
the United States, so we learned to appreciate each other that
year. (Yes, even the sister that I had to share a bedroom with!)

During our one Thanksgiving in our German apartment,
we realized that the oven in the kitchen was too small to
hold the succulent golden turkey that my mother traditionally
prepared for Thanksgiving. Instead, my mother cooked a pre-

packaged turkey roll, which was rather bland. However, she still managed to cook her wonderful side dishes on that tiny three-burner stove. We still fondly recall that Thanksgiving from many years ago, even with its bland turkey roll.

❦ Cathy Fraser

❦

Sunday dinner was a special meal for our family and guests. The meat and desserts varied, but we always used Grandma's recipe for Mashed Potato Filling. The bread was cubed and seasoned first, heaped in an enamel dishpan, and set on the utility cart to dry out a little (a temptation to snack thieves). On Saturday we added mashed potatoes, butter, celery, and seasonings, then placed it in casserole dishes ready to bake.

In the evening, we children put the boards in the long extension table and polished it while Mother ironed the starched tablecloths. On Sunday morning after the food was in the oven, we went to the bedrooms and spread the heirloom quilts on the beds, especially the hand-embroidered and appliqued quilt Grandma had someone make for Dad. It had a farm scene complete with buildings, horses, and a wagon.

❦ Brenda Hochstedler

❦

I don't remember having any birthday or holiday meals at home while I was growing up. We always went next door to Grandma's and Grandpa's house.

It just seemed to be understood. Early every Sunday morning the phone would ring while we were getting ready for church. My brother and I would yell, "We'll be there," before one of my parents answered. Without fail, Grandma and Grandpa, and Ma's single sister who lived with them,

Phyllis sharing food with her grandmother, Anna W. Neff, who hosted her family for most Sunday dinners.

invited us for Sunday dinner. That's where the big meals happened, and everyone seemed happy with that.

I was born one week before Christmas. Grandma was born two weeks before. Grandpa was born one week after New Year's. My aunt was born between new Year's and Grandpa's birthday. We each got our own special meal—no doubling up. In this family we sacrificed no celebrations.

Every year, Grandma asked me what kind of cake I wanted. Every year I said the same thing. "Spice." My final bite was always what I called "a goodie piece," with icing on three sides.

I tell my husband Merle that I was as close to being spoiled as a kid could be—without being spoiled!

🍂 *Phyllis Pellman Good*

Blunders

Although we never did without, we didn't have a lot of money. Mom always made us really nice birthday cakes, but we couldn't afford to buy bakery cakes. The year I turned 10, I waited all day for Mom to start making my birthday cake. I thought my entire family had forgotten my birthday.

I started ranting and raving about how no one loved me and went to the kitchen to make my own birthday cake. I was furious! I was about half through with my cake when my father walked through the door with my presents and the most beautiful bakery cake you have ever seen.

It was my very first bakery cake, and it was stunning! I was so embarrassed at my behavior. I should have known they didn't forget my birthday. The entire family had been laughing behind my back, waiting for the surprise to arrive.

Mollie Burnett

My mother decorated cakes when we were children. She was always baking something for someone. One year my mom made a huge cake for my great-grandmother's birthday. We all piled into the car for the celebration at Granny's house with the cake in the front seat between Mom and Dad, my little brother and I in the back.

We arrived right on time, cake intact—until my little brother jumped over the seat to get out of the car instead of using the back door. He stepped right in the middle of the cake! Well, we took the cake in, my great-grandmother got to see her cake, and then Mom coolly cut out the stepped-in part and proceeded to serve birthday cake. ❧ *DeAnna Wolf*

When I was 9 years old, I really wanted a pair of pompom footie socks. They were all the rage, and I wanted them very badly. My mom finally gave in and bought a pair for me—navy blue with white pompoms and a white rickrack design around the cuff.

I loved those socks. I wanted to wear them everyday, but my mom said they had to be washed out every night if I wanted to do that. One morning before school, I remembered I hadn't hand washed my socks the night before, so I quickly washed them and set them on the top of the toaster to dry. The toast came out perfectly every time, so my 9-year-old brain thought that the socks would, too. Well, unfortunately, the polyester socks melted, and I was left with no pompom footie socks and a pretty irritated mom!   ❧ *Kandi Dodrill*

W hen I was 11 years old, I wanted to surprise Mom and Dad while they were at work by baking a cake from scratch. I forgot a very important ingredient: baking powder. The layer cake came out looking more like a pancake.

I disposed of the disaster in the chicken coop. When my parents came home, they noticed the chickens circling around the coop strangely and upon investigation saw a dead chicken lying next to my cake disaster. My family teased me for this forever! Actually, Dad said he thought the chicken was ill already, and the cake just helped it along.   ❧ *Betty McGuirk*

M y mom and I were fixing Christmas dinner when I was about 9 years old, and I was mashing the potatoes. I reached in the fridge and grabbed what I thought was the milk.

My mom looked over just as I poured Dad's homemade eggnog into the potatoes. She had a fit! But we served them anyway, and everyone asked what we did to the mashed potatoes because they were so tasty. We never did tell.

Now that I am a grandma and my grandkids help in the kitchen, they love when I tell that story.   ❧ *Patricia Bevans*

Once, Mom had to be away from home for the day and left a recipe for me to prepare for the family after I got home from school. One of the ingredients listed on the recipe was a clove of garlic. So I added ground cloves and garlic. It was quite obvious to everyone that my recipe didn't taste like Mom's version of the same. I was mortified.

❧ *Lynn Houston*

❦

I was supposed to fry chicken for supper while my folks were away, and I got a late start because I was visiting with the neighbor kids. I hurried to get the chicken egged and floured and put the grease in the skillet. As I was getting the rest of the supper ready, I noticed the chicken was not cooking—just sitting in the pan.

I turned up the heat as my parents would be home any minute. When my mom walked in the door and watched me turn the first piece of chicken, stringing and burning, she said, "What is this? It's not cooking oil!" I had grabbed the white syrup instead of the oil, and our chicken was very sweet that night. I got a talking-to about my friends hanging around when I was cooking.

❧ *Pam Spiek*

❦

When I was a teenager, our daddy was a rotating shift worker at the diaper plant, and Mama worked the evening shift at the cloth mill. It must have been summer when I remember a couple of my sisters and I walking toward the house at dusk.

Diddy (the name we called our daddy) was sitting on the front steps with the doors and windows open, and smoke was coming out of every opening. He'd fallen asleep while cooking, and the pot had burned and smoked up the entire house. Mama would be home at midnight, so we did our best to air out the house.

But when Mama walked in, the scent hit her nose, and I remember her shaking her head with tears streaming down her face, saying, "James, I've told you about putting food on this stove and then laying down when you know you're going to fall asleep!"

The next day when Mama left for work, Diddy and all six of us kids and a couple of the neighborhood kids got to work scrubbing the smoky ceiling and walls. Diddy went uptown to the local hardware store and purchased paint. We painted like mad.

When Mama walked in just after midnight, the entire house had been painted her go-to color—eggshell. That was thirty-something years ago, and Mama's house is still painted eggshell.   *Deborah Thomas*

❧

My mom wasn't a good cook. She just didn't seem to like doing it. But she did have a summer salad we liked, and it was easy.

She would put a tablespoon of sugar in with sliced onions and cucumbers, and then cover the mixture with vinegar. After a few hours in the refrigerator, she would add tomatoes right before serving.

One time when she had a cold and couldn't smell, she used ammonia instead of vinegar. When the salad came to table, the vegetables were stinking and rotten. From that time on, she never had ammonia in the house.

Roseanna Campbell-Blake

Esther Becker's mother, Anna Hess, checks the turkey as daughter-in-law Lois Hess and her son Phil look on.

When I was an older teen, my mother asked me to make two pumpkin pies with the pumpkin she had taken from the freezer and left sitting on the counter. So I proceeded to make the crusts and mix up the filling. I thought it didn't seem like enough to fill both crusts, so I added more milk and eggs. Then I put the pies in the oven to bake.

A bit later, my mother came into the kitchen. "Esther," she said, "What did you put in the oven? The pumpkin I told you to use is still sitting here on the

Lemon Rice
Esther Becker

1 cup rice
3 cups water, *divided*
grated rind and juice of 2 lemons
¾-1 cup sugar

1. Cook rice in 2 cups water as directed on box.
2. To grated lemon rind and juice, add sugar to taste and remaining one cup water. Add to cooked rice.
3. Let stand overnight in refrigerator before serving. Very refreshing in summer.

counter." No wonder I had to add more ingredients—I had forgotten to include the pumpkin!

"Well," she said, "The pumpkin must be used up. You'll have to make two more pies."

So in the end, we had two pumpkin pies and two spicy custard pies. Of course, my brothers couldn't wait to tell the story to my boyfriend when he came over.　🌿 *Esther Becker*

🌿

One evening my mother was at work, and my sister was cooking pork chops. Of course, I was right there underfoot, standing beside the stove, watching every move my sister made. She flipped over the chops, and some of the hot grease splashed onto my chest.

My sister immediately called Mom, and she came home as fast as she could. Thankfully it wasn't that bad, so Mom fixed me up, and we went out to get ice cream. She said it would help the burn, and it did.　🌿 *Kathy*

🌿

When I was little, my grandmother—who wasn't a very good cook by her own admission—tried to help out my mom and cook dinner before she got home. She planned to fry up some fish in my dad's fryer. My grandmother didn't think to take the plastic top off before heating up the oil, so the plastic melted into the oil and ruined the fryer. Undaunted, my grandmother ordered pizza, so my mom still wouldn't have to cook.　🌿 *Colleen Turner*

🌿

Everyone in our household had an important job to do. Some of us, when we were old enough, would shop for groceries with a list provided by Mom. We learned how to clean bathrooms and fold clothes. All of these chores were supposed to make us responsible. I was the oldest and responsible for a lot of chores in our household.

One memory I have illustrates how much these responsibilities matured me. One afternoon, I heard my best friend, Bobby, screaming at their house next door, so I ran out the back door and over to her house. The stove and the curtain at the window were on fire.

Bobby had panicked, but I just grabbed the baking soda and doused the stove. I tore the curtain down into the sink and turned on the water. By this time the other neighbors in the cul-de-sac had arrived, but the fire was already out.

❧ *Mary Keen*

❧

My mom used to make the most wonderful home-made bread. We had large bay windows in our living room, and Mom would put the bread near those windows to rise. I was fascinated by the process, so she would always let me know when the loaves had risen up high enough to notice the difference.

One day she called from the living room that the bread was rising. I came rushing through the kitchen, only to hit my head on a pull-out cutting board. Mom was horrified, of course, but I still wanted to see the bread.

The cut was deep enough to leave a small scar. Now and again I notice it and think of Mom. I lost her to an accident in 1984, but in some strange way, I still have her with me in that scar—a physical reminder of the love she shared with me through her cooking in that kitchen. ❧ *Rich LaVere*

I was the third child in a pastor's family. This meant that we were often either invited away for Sunday noon meals or that we would have company in our home. On the Sundays that we ate in others' homes, my mother would often remind us children en route to "always be polite, even if the food doesn't look or taste like what we eat at home."

One day, we observed my mother practicing what she taught us. A lady gave Mom a plateful of homemade meat pies. This lady was so proud of what she had made, and Mom graciously accepted the gift. The lady, her children, and her home were filthy, and there was no way that Mom could feed "food made in that house" to her family. We never saw those meat pies on our table.

Several days later, the lady stopped by our house and asked Mom what she thought of the pies. Mom replied, "Food like that doesn't last long at our house!" To this day, Mom won't tell us what she did with the pies, but we suspect that the pigs enjoyed them. *Anita Troyer*

One time before bed, Mother forgot to turn off the hot water faucet in the bathroom sink above the kitchen. In the morning, the floor was flooded with water running down the kitchen walls and dripping from the ceiling. What a mess! It meant taking off the wallpaper and replacing the linoleum, which had buckled. It was an expensive way to change the kitchen decor. *A. Catherine Boshart*

I wanted to surprise Mom one day. When she got home from work, I was making a simple supper—mixing butter into some macaroni and cheese.

My little brother, age 4 at the time, was setting the table. All of a sudden the lights in the kitchen and the living room dimmed. Mom came running to see what happened, just in time to see my brother flying across the room. He had stuck a fork into one of the outlets in the wall. He was only allowed to set the table with spoons for a while after that!

🌺 *April Christian*

E very summer my mother would dry some sweet corn. After the corn was cut off the cob, she propped a ladder on the lower side of the slanted roof of the chicken house and laid a linen table cloth on the hot tin. Mother would spread gallons of corn out evenly on the table cloth on a summer's day.

The starch in the corn caused it to stick to the cloth, and it needed to be scraped loose with a knife quite frequently in order for it to dry evenly. On one particularly hot day in the 1960s, Mother let out a holler when she climbed the ladder to stir the corn. "All that work, and look what happened!" she cried.

Most of the corn had burned. I remember trying to save the day by meticulously separating the burnt corn from the dried corn, but in the end there was very little that was salvageable.

🌺 *June S. Groff*

Ordinary Times

My six siblings and I would play outside. We didn't have an air conditioner, so the windows were always open. The scent of something frying would float out of the windows to the backyard. The smell of good food can be just as good as the meal itself, I think.

Back then we could eat fried foods without gaining weight because we played outside all day—kickball, baseball, dodgeball, basketball with a wire hoop even though the net was long gone.

There was no snacking between meals. I remember standing in the kitchen next to the wall crying because the pork chops or chicken Mama was frying smelled so good, and, shoot, I was hungry! Mama would always shake her head and say, "Debbie, I'm going as fast as I can!"

For dessert, Diddy (the name we called our daddy) would always bring home Little Debbie cakes or Moon Pies.

❧ *Deborah Thomas*

The whole family sat down together for every meal. I remember we always had hot cocoa for breakfast, year round. We might have eggs, toast, or cereal but rarely pancakes. Before each breakfast, we had family devotions with Bible reading and prayer.

The noon meal was the biggest meal of the day—a full meat-and-potatoes farmer's dinner. Supper was lighter. In summer when berries were in season, we might have corn pone with the fruit and milk. If watermelons were ripe, that might have been the main part of a supper. ❧ *Esther Becker*

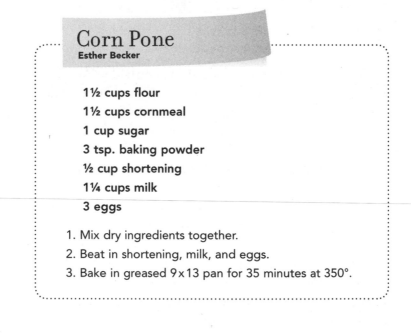

Corn Pone
Esther Becker

1½ cups flour
1½ cups cornmeal
1 cup sugar
3 tsp. baking powder
½ cup shortening
1¼ cups milk
3 eggs

1. Mix dry ingredients together.
2. Beat in shortening, milk, and eggs.
3. Bake in greased 9 x 13 pan for 35 minutes at 350°.

My mother always cooked because my father had one meal that he could make: hot dogs and beans. I grew up hating fish, but we had fish often because Mom would bring them home from work (she's a marine biologist). They'd catch the fish off the boats in the nets during their experiments.

The meals I remember best were things like beef stir fry and beef stroganoff (both made from the previous night's roast beef meal), lasagna, spaghetti (always different according to the vegetables she added from the garden), quiche, and roast chicken. All of them were basic comfort food meals, but they were especially delicious to me because they weren't fish!

Since there were six people in our family and my mother always cooked just enough for six people with small appetites, mealtime was a contest to get enough to eat. One night my mother had placed everything except for her tea on the table. When she returned with her tea, all the food was eaten. That is when saying grace was instituted in our household. Mom still did not make larger amounts of food, and I never knew why.   ❧ *A. MacPhee*

Recently Mama told me about how she went back to work when I was a toddler. One day when she came home, I ran into her legs crying, "Mama's home, Mama's home!" She gave her two-week notice the next day. I really don't remember that.

What I do remember is that Mama was always at home and wore pretty house dresses. The ones I remember had ruffles and wrapped around the front and tied with a big bow in the back.

And she was pretty. At one time she was encouraged to become a model for Neiman Marcus. She told me that as she waited in line to be interviewed at Neiman's, she reasoned that if she became a model, she would not have time to have children, and she wanted children. So she stepped out of line, caught the bus, and went home.

Our home, three blocks from my school, always smelled good when I got home. Mama would open the door and lead me into the kitchen where there would be a piece of still-warm cake and a glass of cold milk ready as my after school snack.

Delicious food cooking in the kitchen was the perfume of the house. We didn't have Scentsy back then, and we didn't need it. The smell of fried chicken, mashed potatoes and gravy, chocolate cake, and lemon pie is what home smells like to me.

There was a kind of rhythm to the menu because of Daddy's travel schedule. Those few days without our father became the time of menu change. Mama would make all the things that she liked, but Daddy didn't. So we would gorge ourselves on huge mounds of homemade fried onion rings. To this day, nobody—and I do mean nobody—makes onion rings like Mama did when I was growing up. Even my older sister agrees with me on that. There were also homemade corn dogs, fried eggplant, and liberal use of real butter and raw onions when Daddy was away.

I learned to cook a little while watching her and helping in the kitchen. When I was really little, I remember wanting to cook. Mama would give me a big bowl and a spoon and let me use any ingredient in the kitchen to create something. The only rule was that I couldn't use it all up. I'm pretty fearless in the kitchen now. I credit my mom with that.

Oh, Mama. You're the best!   ❧ *Diane Blaising*

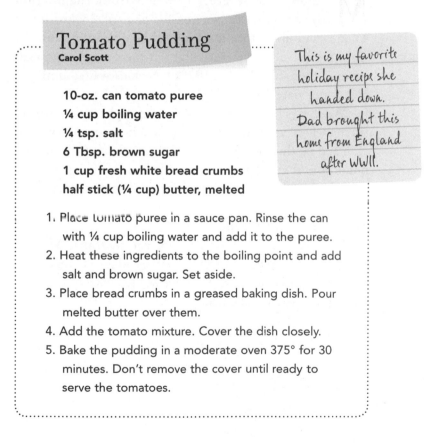

Mom was pretty strict on two mealtime issues. First, we had to have breakfast before leaving for school or work (Dad, too!). Secondly, Sunday afternoon dinner we all had to be there and have dinner together.

Other than those two rules, we could watch TV in the living room or sit at the table. Mom served food at the table in casserole dishes or bowls. It made even small meals look like more, and I think she knew that.

My family didn't talk much at the table. I wish I had known to ask more questions about their childhoods and their dreams. **✖** *Carol Scott*

Tomato Pudding
Carol Scott

This is my favorite holiday recipe she handed down. Dad brought this home from England after WWII.

10-oz. can tomato puree
¼ cup boiling water
¼ tsp. salt
6 Tbsp. brown sugar
1 cup fresh white bread crumbs
half stick (¼ cup) butter, melted

1. Place tomato puree in a sauce pan. Rinse the can with ¼ cup boiling water and add it to the puree.
2. Heat these ingredients to the boiling point and add salt and brown sugar. Set aside.
3. Place bread crumbs in a greased baking dish. Pour melted butter over them.
4. Add the tomato mixture. Cover the dish closely.
5. Bake the pudding in a moderate oven 375° for 30 minutes. Don't remove the cover until ready to serve the tomatoes.

My mother is European, so she was so beautiful and exotic compared to other moms I knew. She gardened, and we picked mushrooms, berries, and dandelions for wine. She made her own bread and wine. We did not eat sandwiches like other kids. We had meat, cheese, and hot peppers with a piece of rye bread on the side.　*Beth Sexton*

My mom was severely crippled from rheumatoid arthritis from the age of 13. She still cooked for us six kids and up to four roomers and boarders for a total of eight to twelve people every night. If there was not enough room at the table, the youngest of the kids waited until the older ones were finished.

We always had complete meals every night with meat and three or four vegetables. Saturday was homemade soups or chili and sandwiches. Sunday was always fried chicken, corn, potatoes and gravy, and a tossed salad.

We always had lemonade, sweetened with saccharin for my oldest brother who had diabetes. We had skimmed milk made from powdered milk.

We were never allowed to not eat anything. My dad believed it was an insult to Mom, so we had to eat everything. We always had as much bread as we wanted with apple butter and always had a homemade dessert.　*C. Kay Browning*

Whichever child was hanging around the kitchen at suppertime got to go to the pantry and pick out two cans of vegetables to round out the meal. I liked to choose one can of corn and one can of peas—bright, pretty colors for our plates. Sometimes we would have cranberry jelly—the type that slides out of a can—and we kids would dare one another to take a sip of milk after a bite of cranberry. So sour!

Every Saturday, mom served either fish cakes and baked beans (both pea and kidney beans) or hot dogs grilled in a cast iron pan with lots of butter and beans. Ironically, I married a man who is allergic to fish and beans, so I only feed my memories with these dishes when he's out of town!

Mom was very sympathetic about our food preferences and tried to accommodate us to a reasonable degree. This was because—she told us—as a child she was once forced to remain at the table until she cleaned her plate, including a piece of gristly meat that grew colder and more inedible by the minute. She couldn't do it.

Cruelly, my grandmother made hot buttered popcorn—a treat she never prepared, ordinarily—and served it to everyone but my mom. Though we loved our grandma, we were upset by this unfairness, and we empathized with the little girl who became our mom.

Marie Verge Davis, Linda's mother, dressed for winter weather in Massachusetts in 1955 a few years before Linda was born.

So, if we didn't care for whatever was being served (and I remember trying hard to like everything), my mother would simply say, "There's cereal in the cupboard or bologna in the fridge; help yourself." I would get myself a big bowl of

Cheerios or a bologna sandwich on liver-and-onions night. That way we could all dine together, enjoying each other's company, and know that our own tastes were respected.

❧ *Linda Davis Siess*

❦

Mom always cooked. I joked that Daddy could mess up a peanut butter sandwich. It was true! He always pushed too hard with the knife and had the bread in crumbs.

The favorite foods that I remember most from growing up were baked chicken, baked steak, steak on the grill with baked potatoes, and roast beef in the Crockpot. We didn't eat a lot of pasta, because Daddy didn't like it and then Mom would have had to fix him something else. ❧ *Sara Harris*

❦

My mom did most of the cooking, but when she worked nights, Dad would do it—usually something simple, like grilled cheese, hot dogs, or sloppy joes.

Mom cooked on weekends, and she never made us eat anything she herself or Dad didn't like. Many times peas were served, and I was permitted to play with my food then—hiding the peas in mashed potatoes—because my parents knew if I couldn't see them, I would eat them.

The television was never on during meals. Dad saw to that; he said meals were family time and that the boob tube took away from that. At our table, we kids were encouraged to talk about our days—unless my grandparents were at the dinner table. Then children were seen, not heard, unless specifically spoken to. ❧ *Kathy Workman*

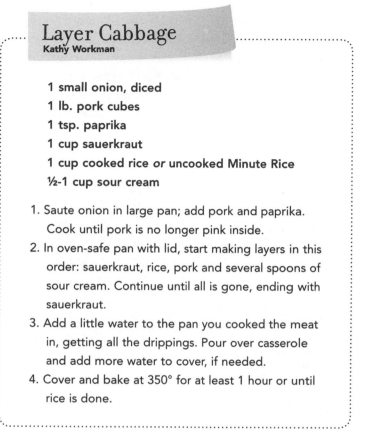

Layer Cabbage
Kathy Workman

1 small onion, diced
1 lb. pork cubes
1 tsp. paprika
1 cup sauerkraut
1 cup cooked rice *or* uncooked Minute Rice
½-1 cup sour cream

1. Saute onion in large pan; add pork and paprika. Cook until pork is no longer pink inside.
2. In oven-safe pan with lid, start making layers in this order: sauerkraut, rice, pork and several spoons of sour cream. Continue until all is gone, ending with sauerkraut.
3. Add a little water to the pan you cooked the meat in, getting all the drippings. Pour over casserole and add more water to cover, if needed.
4. Cover and bake at 350° for at least 1 hour or until rice is done.

E very Wednesday evening, my mother-in-law would mix up a large bowl filled with enough dough to make nine loaves of bread. It would rise all night, and the next morning it was formed into loaves and popped in the oven. Her two older sons stopped on their way home from work to pick up their weekly "rations."

She welcomed a new baby with a piggy bank that had one penny in it and a loaf of bread. Her bread was given for any special occasion.

The only time we ate in front of the TV at her house was Sunday night when the meal consisted of hot chocolate and buttered fresh bread. This is, in fact, a favorite of my children and grandchildren, although we often forget to do it. Life gets complicated and busy, and we often forget the good things from our past.   *Carol Findling*

***

I liked drying dishes while Ma washed. She and Dad built our house in the late '50s, modeling it after a place they had spotted in a nearby town. But Ma always regretted that she hadn't insisted on a few things about the kitchen that bugged her forever.

She yearned for a dishwasher. But she had filled every inch of cupboard space, so she could never figure out what to give up to make space for the thing. So we washed and dried dishes by hand. Dad thought that was good for my brother and me.

Ma and I had a routine when she and I were the dishwashing team. She'd say the name of a family we both knew, and I'd say the kind of car they drove. I had memorized the make and model of all our friends' and relatives' cars, plus my grandparents' friends. Grandma and Grandpa lived next door, so I saw their visitors' cars all the time.

Phyllis, right, at about age 3, and her next-door neighbor friend, Doris, raid Grandma Neff's stove drawer for snacks.

I have no idea why that fascinated me so much, but Ma was a great partner, because I realize now that she had to memorize all of them, too!   ❧ *Phyllis Pellman Good*

❧

Mom cooked just about every night. Some of my favorite dishes were chicken and rice, spaghetti and meatballs, fish sticks, and skinny pancakes (crepes) that we would spread with jelly and roll up.

I also loved chip-and-dip night. Chip-and-dip night consisted of cottage cheese with potato chips, a tomato stuffed with tuna salad, and hard-cooked eggs. Only on a rare occasion did we not sit at the dinner table. Watching The Wizard of Oz and eating tacos on dinner trays was a treat!

    ❧ *Nancy Johnson*

❧

We all sat down together at the table, even for breakfast, and waited to start eating until the food was blessed. I especially have warm, cozy memories of coming down from our upstairs bedrooms on winter mornings, welcomed by the smell of moua (stomach) balsam tea that Mom had harvested from outside the back door and then frozen for just such mornings with the window sills arched with new snow and the kitchen made all the more quiet and cozy by the dark cold outside.

It brings tears to my eyes even now and a longing to do it again that I guess can never be satisfied (except through memories) when I think of those quiet winter mornings. I, and sometimes my sister, would stand on a stool between the warm stove and the cupboard and watch Mom stir the bubbling oatmeal with raisins and steep the morning tea leaves in hot water. We were comfortable not talking, and she might hum a little tune.

I felt ready to face another day at school after those connecting times, knowing that she'd be the same calm person all day, keeping a clean house for us, and watching for us when we came home again. I especially felt that way, realizing that some of my friends didn't know what they'd face when they got home.

By contrast, our supper times were more lively with discussions about the events of the day—all in Pennsylvania Dutch. I remember one time when I wanted to use some new vocabulary that I had learned on the school playground, and I said that my finger "hurt like the Dickens," and my mom and dad just about lost their mouthfuls! And so meal times were times of learning the finer things of life, too!

Oh, and Bob Andy pie, and the salmon patties with the bones left in as treasures for us to find, and our Saturday night Chef Boyardee pizza kits that came in a box. Pizza was a new modern food then, so they sold kits with crust ingredient packages, a little can of pizza sauce, and a packet of Parmesan cheese. We added the hamburger and Velveeta cheese, and we

Marlene's parents, LeRoy and Anna (Miller) Schrock, in December 1965 on their 25th wedding anniversary. This was in the kitchen of their house in northern Wisconsin.

The house was set back in a long lane right up against a big woods of mostly tall pine trees, where deer roamed and chipmunks scampered freely. Most of Marlene's childhood friends were the black-haired Native American children that lived around her and went to school with her.

thought that was so good—just that! Nowadays, that hardly touches all the toppings that are available. ✒ *Marlene Graber*

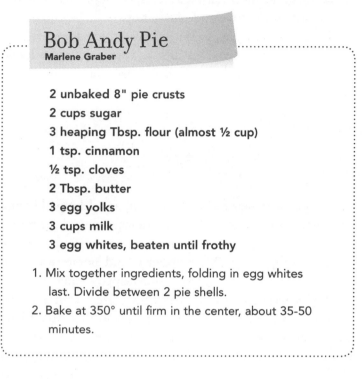

Bob Andy Pie
Marlene Graber

2 unbaked 8" pie crusts
2 cups sugar
3 heaping Tbsp. flour (almost ½ cup)
1 tsp. cinnamon
½ tsp. cloves
2 Tbsp. butter
3 egg yolks
3 cups milk
3 egg whites, beaten until frothy

1. Mix together ingredients, folding in egg whites last. Divide between 2 pie shells.
2. Bake at 350° until firm in the center, about 35-50 minutes.

M y mom was a simple woman. She never had a lot of material stuff, but she made do with what she did have. She was a genius in finding materials to make me school clothes, and I must say I was an original in them.

In the same way, she liked to see what kinds of dishes she could fix with whatever she had in her kitchen, and we never went away from her table hungry. If company showed up, I think her food grew like the loaves and fishes in the Bible. Dad was a fisherman, so fried fish was a staple at our house.

Her best food in the world to make for us kids was chocolate gravy and homemade biscuits. My mom made us chocolate gravy for breakfast at least five days a week. It was economical at the time and filled us up.

I was the only girl, so we did everything together. She taught me how to make biscuits, and we practiced a lot so I could try to get them right. But to this day, I can't find a better biscuit or make one even close to hers.

❧ *Leslie Johnson*

Grandma always did the cooking, and I helped some. In the summertime, there were always fresh sliced tomatoes on the table, some sort of homemade bread, biscuits, or cornbread, and fresh green beans and potatoes cooked together from the garden that I had helped gather.

My grandfather would drink his coffee from a saucer because it was usually too hot for him, and that would help cool it down. We would talk about what needed to be done in the garden, how good supper was, and what happened during our day.

❧ *Hazel Anderson*

My father was a foreman at the Bethlehem Steel plant, and he worked different shifts. When he was on night or day shifts, we could all sit down at the kitchen table at 5 p.m. and eat our meal together as a family. School days meant I had to finish my homework before I could help my mother in the kitchen. That was always incentive to get my homework done!

My mother always liked to cook, and she made sure we had a cooked meal every night. As I grew a little older, around 10 or 11 years old, I would sit at the kitchen table and watch her cook.

Before long, I got the job of peeling the potatoes for the fried potatoes that we had every night. This was a favorite of my father's. No matter what else we had for dinner, we *always* had to have fried potatoes. They had to be "sliced" with the potato peeler so they would be nice, paper-thin pieces.

On rare occasions, my father made his delicious home-made spaghetti sauce. I remember him grating carrots to put in the sauce, something that was quite unusual in the '50s and '60s! This was way before Julia Child opened our eyes to adventure in the kitchen! His spaghetti sauce was the best.

❦ Susan Bickta

❦

G rowing up in Alaska, we had an unbelievable array of wildlife, and Dad would try to get his gang of seven children to appreciate the food. We did have the usual fish sticks and minute steaks sometimes, but I also remember whole salmons that my parents would buy from the Eskimos in the Fairbanks area. Mom would bring the whole fish home, fillet it, and then cover the salmon with bacon to cook it. There is nothing to compare to that simple straight cooking.

We always sat down together in the small government-housing dining area right next to the kitchen. The stove was so close to the table that when we left the door open it would heat the whole area.

❦ Mary Keen

❦

S pecial times that stand out to me, believe it or not, were when we did dishes together. I hated trying to tackle the mounds of hardened food and unidentifiable objects on the eating wares, so Mom would take pity on me and say that she would wash while I could dry. Dad would be working, and my brother would be outside, so we had the whole time to ourselves to just talk and talk and talk.

We solved all of the world's problems and laughed and cried together. I remember struggling with issues or things that my friends would say and waiting until dishwashing time to talk about it with Mom. Whenever I pick up a dish towel, I forever remember Mom! ❧ *MarJanita Geigley*

Portuguese Sausage Soup

MarJanita Geigley
Makes 6 side-dish servings

4 oz. hot Italian sausage links sliced ¼-inches thick
4 oz. sweet Italian sausage links sliced ¼-inches thick
half an onion, chopped
½ cup water
2 medium potatoes, peeled and sliced
2 14½-oz. cans chicken *or* vegetable broth
10-oz. pkg. frozen spinach
¼ tsp. pepper
2 cups barley

1. In a large saucepan, cook the hot sausage, sweet sausage, and onion until sausage is browned and onion is tender; drain fat.
2. Add potatoes, broth, barley, spinach, water, and pepper. Bring to boil.
3. Reduce heat; cover and simmer for about 20 minutes or until potatoes are tender.

We ate this one time at a restaurant and loved it, so Mom got the recipe and proceeded to way outdo the previous soup!

＄ᒚ

When I was a small girl back in the '50s, we had our own chickens. Whenever we had extra eggs that needed to be used up, my mother would make noodles.

I came home from school one day, and she was just finishing up rolling out the dough. I watched her cut them expertly and precisely. She picked up the cutting board with the golden yellow noodles, and I followed her into her bedroom. There on the bed were more noodles than I had ever seen, lying on colorful feed sacks that she had sewed together. She gently pushed the noodles off of the board onto a bare corner of the sacks to dry. She had been making noodles for most of the day.

Back in the kitchen, I helped my mother clean up and dried the dishes. I asked her why she was making so many noodles. She told me that several people had asked if they could buy her noodles, and she was excited to earn some extra money as a stay-at-home mom. Well, my mother's noodle business grew, and in time, every bed would be covered with the golden noodles when she made them.

＄ *Kathleen S. Robertson*

＄ᒚ

Mealtime in my house was an exercise in routine. You could set your watch to it.

I would arrive home from school on the bus promptly at 4:00 p.m. First, I would bring in the laundry hanging out to dry on the washline, and as I was folding it, I enjoyed the few blissful minutes of being home alone watching television programs.

Then the phone would ring. Mom was calling from work to provide instructions for preparing dinner. These instructions had been given once already that day when she woke me up for school, but this was a friendly reminder to cut through the morning haze and ensure that dinner was hot and ready by the time Dad got home.

I could not cook, and neither could my brother or dad, for the kitchen was Mom's world—not out of any gender role duty but because she loved to cook. So for me, dinner preparation did not involve measuring ingredients or chopping or anything resembling what a chef might do. It was simply hitting the button on the oven for 350 degrees, moving a casserole dish from the fridge to the oven, and setting the timer for the appropriate amount of time.

Unfortunately, even this basic task was occasionally easier said than done. I will never live down the day when a pan full of party chicken sat for 90 minutes in a cold oven that I had forgotten to turn on while I played video games. I believe I lost that privilege for a couple of days after that!

At 5:00 on the dot, Mom would come home from work, take a shower, prepare any side dishes that needed some help, and set the table before Dad arrived.

By 6:00, Dad was home. If he was running even five minutes late, he would call and explain.

I have particularly fond memories of the long, cold evenings of wintertime. I remember sitting by the window—stomach rumbling—looking out into the darkness, and waiting to see the lights of his car turn into our driveway so I could turn on the radio and run to my seat for dinner. The cold air coming in from outside as he opened the door and hugged us was neutralized by the warmth emanating from the kitchen and the sweet smells of bread crumbs, melted cheese, and roasted chicken coming from inside.   ✖ *Ben Cattell Noll*

One of my most cherished pictures is one of my mom, her mom, and me cooking an *old* favorite: mush. It sounds gross, but it tastes like heaven! My great-grandmother said mush was a staple during the Depression because it was cheap and filling. 🍃 *Angel Skelton*

Mush
Angel Skelton

1. Fix up 3 cups of water in a pan to boil. Mix 1 cup cornmeal with 1 cup cold water. When the water in the pan is boiling, slowly pour in the cornmeal/water mixture, stirring constantly.
2. Cook as though you are making grits (low, with the lid on), making sure to stir often so as to not have lumps. Add some salt to taste (about 2 tsp.). When cooked thoroughly and smooth, about 20 minutes, pour into a loaf-style bread pan. Cover and put in fridge overnight.
3. Flip hardened mixture out on wax paper and slice in about ¼-inch slices. Dredge each slice in additional cornmeal and fry in about 1½ inches of corn oil in a large black iron skillet. You don't want the oil to cover the slices, just enough to be able to brown.
4. When each slice is golden brown on each side, it's done. Keep warm and serve with warm syrup, like pancakes. Wonderful with thick-sliced bacon.

O ne of my favorite times to be in Mother's kitchen was on a cold winter evening. When the snow was quietly falling outside and the sun had gone to bed early, the kitchen was a welcoming place to be.

The savory aroma of chicken corn noodle soup would scent the air, while fresh applesauce bubbled on the back burner. Whole wheat muffins, topped with cinnamon or sprinkled with sugar, would be baking in the oven, ready to come out when Daddy came home. A green leaf salad was always served in a pretty glass bowl. Sometimes there were whole red beets or squash to add as a side dish.

The dinner table would be set according to Mother's instructions: "Spoons on the right, forks on the left." We had to do it correctly and also neatly, for Mother was a perfectionist!

I remember how the windows would get fogged over from the warm, steamy kitchen, and we'd wipe a spot clear as we waited for Daddy's car. When he arrived, Mother would call us all to the table, and we'd sit down to a feast of food and love.   🛥 *Sara Meyers*

☙

T he summer before my senior year in high school, we moved into a two-bedroom apartment from a twenty-room judge's estate that had been turned into a children's home where my parents had worked. There were six of us all together, and the apartment was cozy.

Mom had to learn how to cook all over again because we had a cook at the children's home. Mom was always experimenting with something, and I grew to dread coming home from school and hearing, "I made a new invention!" Somehow the inventions in her head never really came together the way I think she imagined them. But she never stopped trying.

My favorite dish from this time was her staple—simple tuna noodle casserole. One time we sat around the table together, talking and laughing, wondering why this time the casserole tasted so different. She had forgotten to add the tuna! Oh my. 	 ❧ *Lisa Wolfe*

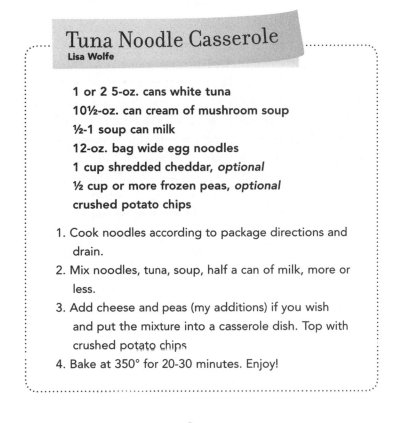

Tuna Noodle Casserole
Lisa Wolfe

1 or 2 5-oz. cans white tuna
10½-oz. can cream of mushroom soup
½-1 soup can milk
12-oz. bag wide egg noodles
1 cup shredded cheddar, *optional*
½ cup or more frozen peas, *optional*
crushed potato chips

1. Cook noodles according to package directions and drain.
2. Mix noodles, tuna, soup, half a can of milk, more or less.
3. Add cheese and peas (my additions) if you wish and put the mixture into a casserole dish. Top with crushed potato chips
4. Bake at 350° for 20-30 minutes. Enjoy!

We always sat down together at the table when we ate. We each had our own places to sit according to our ages. On Sunday night, we children took turns bringing up the quart jar of canned fruit that we liked best.

My sisters and I would sing from a songbook placed

above the sink while we did the supper dishes. One time the songbook fell in the dish water. We still remember that to this day, and it happened decades ago.   ❧ *Janet L. Roggie*

❧

M y dad was the everyday cook in the house. He made all meals and even snacks. My mom cooked on her days off or for special occasions. Dad made simple stir fries and stews that didn't require many ingredients and were easy to prepare. Mom made time-consuming things like lumpia—a Filipino egg roll with ground pork and a whole host of vegetables.

Dad shooed us out of the kitchen, but Mom asked for our help. We spent hours talking about her childhood as we spooned filling into wrappers and carefully rolled up the egg rolls into cigar shapes. Sometimes the radio would play in the background, and she would sing Billy Joel songs about being in love with uptown girls.

When everything was rolled and fried to perfection, we would all sit together with a big bowl of white rice and eat the lumpia. My brother would hand me his filling (my favorite), and I'd hand him my fried wrapper (his favorite).

❧ *Michelle Pascua*

❧

M y mother, who had been raised in a strict Amish family, had been taught it was wrong to celebrate birthdays. It was giving too much recognition to one person. She never planned birthday meals or baked birthday cakes that I can remember.

One evening my family was invited to and attended an extended family member's birthday party on my dad's side of the family. When we returned from the party, my mother's small chicken house full of baby chicks had burned down. I remember Mother lamenting having gone to a birthday party. This experience made a deep impression on me, but it did not deter me in any way from loving birthday celebrations.

Mother was one of the most frugal persons I ever knew. Because we had a year's supply of maple syrup on hand, our school lunches usually included at least one sandwich made with this syrup and peanut butter. By noon, this sandwich, wrapped in bread wrapping paper, was usually soaked. The soaked sandwich and the bread wrapping paper was embarrassing to me. My friends' bologna sandwiches were wrapped neatly in fresh wax paper.

At times, Mother would buy cheap bologna for one of our sandwiches—always a treat. However, she never bought the coveted potato chips I saw in some of my friends' lunches. Mostly she would use whatever we had on hand, such as home-canned fruit put in small jam jars with lids.

❧ *Elena Yoder*

❧

When my mother made her version of southern fried chicken, it was not fried. She browned about twenty pieces of chicken and then put it in a heavy-bottom roasting pan and cooked it the oven. Because chicken for nine people was a difficult thing to make, it was something we would have about once a year.

Years later, after my dad passed, I found out that my mother *hated* chicken. Her granddad had a chicken farm, and they ate chicken almost every day during the Depression. She also had the job of candling the eggs. If she had *never* seen another chicken, it would have been too soon!

❧ *Dianne Krumm*

My mother was a busy lady. We lived on a farm in West Virgina. She milked cows, fed chickens, and did gardening plus housework and cooking. I had three sisters and a brother. There were eight of us at meals with the hired man.

There was no electricity in our area back then. We had our own powerhouse with a lot of batteries to power electric lights in the house and barn.

We hung clothes on a line outside to dry. We heated our irons on the cook stove. Instead of a refrigerator, we set things in the spring in our milk house to keep really cold. When I was in high school, we finally got electricity in our area and got a refrigerator.

We walked three quarters of a mile to school most days. In winter snow, Papa sometimes took us on a sled with horses. Sometimes we walked on top of snow drifts when the snow was rather hard and crusty. Once my brother went through the drift, and when my older sister and I pulled him out, his boot came off.

When we came home from school, Mamma had often been baking, and she had a warm treat for us—warm cinnamon rolls just out of the oven or peach cobbler.

We had buckwheat pancakes a lot for breakfast. Mamma started it with yeast and saved a bit each time. At night she added more buckwheat flour and some milk and or water, and in the morning, it had risen and maybe run over the top of the crock—ready for breakfast. ❧ *Elsie Russett*

Learning to Cook

My first experience with cooking was scrambling eggs. I was probably 8 or so, and I was in 4-H. That was one of the tasks that was assigned. Mom went over the instructions to make sure I understood them. She taught me how to crack the eggs and turn on the stove. And she let me at it.

When it looked like I was having trouble, Mom suggested something to make it easier: instead of stirring, I was to run the spatula back and forth while the eggs were cooking. Every time now that I am cooking eggs, I think of that advice. Back and forth my spatula goes, and a smile appears on my face.

❧ *Jill Adams*

When I was 12 and my sister 14, Mom started having us make supper one night a week by ourselves. We were often allowed to experiment with one or two recipes that we had never tried before, but we also had to make something foolproof so that the whole meal wouldn't be a disaster.

Shelley Burns, left, and her younger sister baking together.

My earliest recollection of baking was when I was ten. My mom had been taken to the emergency room and we were waiting for her to come home. I wanted to have something special for her when she came home, so I decided to make her a shoo-fly pie. I had never made a pie before, but I remembered watching Mom make pie crust with the fancy edges. I got out a cookbook and got to work. By the time Mom got home from the hospital, there were two wet-bottom shoo-fly pies waiting for her. *Shelley Burns*

My father was a cook in the Army, and my mother was pretty much raised in the diners that my grandmother ran, so both parents taught me to cook. Dad taught the simple things: eggs, toast, cheese sandwiches, anything from a can. Mom was just happy when I wanted to help in the kitchen, because my two older sisters didn't want to and my younger sister was too little.

I was about 7 when I got one of those little toy ovens that bake tiny little cakes. I couldn't burn myself on those because they didn't unlock until they were totally cooled. Mom would let me have a little cake batter to make a cake or a few plops of cookie dough to make tiny cookies. Then I turned 8 and was permitted to help with the big people's goodies.

Easy Baked Macaroni and Cheese

Kathy Workman

2 cups macaroni
2 tsp. salt
8 oz. Velveeta cheese, cut into small pieces
1½ cups milk
butter
flour

1. Cook macaroni in boiling salted water until almost done, 10-12 minutes; drain well.
2. In a 2-quart casserole, layer the macaroni and cheese, adding a little flour to each layer. End with macaroni on top.
3. Add milk. Dot top with butter.
4. Put into preheated 350° oven and bake approximately 30 minutes, or until top starts to get brown.

Then came the age of 10 and cooking dinner—baked mac and cheese. There are so many different things Mom let me cook after that, but it's the first baked mac and cheese that really started it all. ❧ *Kathy Workman*

❧

I remember the first night everyone came home, and we sat and ate a fabulous meal that I had cooked by myself: meatloaf with mashed potatoes and fresh green beans. When dinner was over, everyone was congratulating me on a great meal.

My mom piped up and said, "Janet dear, I am so proud of you, but next time you make fresh green beans, make sure you snip the ends off of them."

My dad said, "OH, ANN!"

And Mom said, "She needs to learn!"

I have never forgotten that. ❧ *Jan McDonough*

❧

My mother is old-school. She picks mushrooms carefully with a guide book—a self-taught mycophagist. She's a biologist, and she applies her knowledge to flora, fauna, and food. I accompanied her on her foraging trips throughout my life, preferring nature to people because of this. We found grapes, apples, mushrooms, and blueberries on our searches. We stopped the car spontaneously if the weather or area looked right. And this encouraged my desire to cook.

Growing up during World War II gave my mother the impulse to conserve. Leftovers in our house were not thrown out unless they were borderline decomposing. I was taught to smell things to determine their state. I was taught where to look for free edibles and to be curious in other regions about any possible edibles that they had naturally.

Mom canned, steamed, froze, and cooked anything she deemed consumable. We lived near the ocean, so I learned how to pick a lobster for more than its tail meat, to steam quahogs, and to catch razor clams. Mom filleted any kind of fish that she caught during her experiments as a marine biologist. She plucked local ducks, and when one had an undeveloped egg in it, she excitedly called us over to show us. She also skinned rabbits and prepared them for our meals.

Back when school was actually teaching practical skills, I had home economics class. One year, my homework was cooking. I had to make different kinds of recipes and, at the end, cook a full meal for my family. I flubbed once while baking a beautiful apple cake. The horrible taste betrayed my use of salt instead of sugar.

The meal, though, was a success: oven-fried chicken with corn, cranberry sauce, and popovers. My mother was astounded that I had made the popovers so well without cast iron popover pans. I'd told her I was making muffins.

❦ A. MacPhee

❦

Growing up in India, we had servants who did the cooking. But when I came to the States at age 15, my mother thought I should learn to make pie crusts.

The idea for a perfect pie crust came from my grandmother who grew up making pies in Doylestown, PA. The crimping of the edges needed to be just right. It was one way for a single-crust pie and a different way for double-crust pie.

❦ Laverne Nafziger

I loved watching my mom make bread. Mom was a talker when she made bread, especially at Christmastime. She would talk about growing up, how she took care of her younger sister, playing the piano and singing. I learned a lot about my mother during those times. I also learned how to knead bread dough; she always said her arms were tired and I should give it a shot. Now I know it was her hands-on way of teaching me how to do it. We made quite a team, making the red and green Christmas bread! **❧** *Kathy Workman*

Kolach
Kathy Workman

1½ cup lukewarm milk
½ cup sugar
2 packages (2 Tbsp.) dry yeast
½ cup warm water
2 eggs
½ cup shortening
7-7½ cups sifted flour

1. Put yeast in warm water but do not stir. Allow to sit for 5 minutes.
2. In a large bowl, mix milk and sugar. Add yeast and water. Stir briefly.
3. Add flour and mix with a spoon.
4. Knead well. Grease the bowl and the ball of dough. Cover the bowl with a kitchen towel and let rise until double, about 2 hours.
5. Punch down, knead well again and cover again. Let rise a second time, about 1½ hours.

6. After second rising, divide into 2 well-greased 9x5 loaf pans. Cover and let rise a third time until doubled, about 30 minutes.
7. Bake in 350° oven 45-60 minutes or until looks/ thumps done.
8. Cool in pan 10 minutes, then turn onto wire rack to finish cooling.

⁂

My mom taught me to cook when I asked her if I could help. At first, it was to stir the batter or frost a cake. If I did not help, I could not lick the spoon or beaters. I was 8 years old when Mom started to have me help in the kitchen on a regular basis.

The first thing my mom had me make by myself was a pan of brownies when I was 11 years old. Mom insisted that if I was to learn to cook, it had to be from scratch. When I turned 13, Mom required me to fix one meal a week—the whole meal from scratch including a dessert. Since Mom was happy with my help and thought that every kid should learn to cook, she did the same thing with my siblings who followed. I was the oldest of eight children, and some of them still blame me for them having to cook as kids.

❧ *Frank Hemenway*

⁂

Hooray for *Betty Crocker's Boys and Girls Cookbook*. My copy is from sometime in the 1960s—a revised edition of the 1957 volume. I must have received it as a birthday or Christmas present sometime before my ninth birthday, but the best gift was that my mom apparently had confidence in my budding kitchen abilities and left me alone to test, try, and learn.

Nobody ever hovered over me in the kitchen or made a fuss about sharp knives or hot ovens or saucepans full of boiling sugar. I guess my parents figured that I was sensible, practical, a good reader, and skilled at following directions.

Because my mother was in charge of dinner, I happily filled in elsewhere with snacks and desserts. My two most-used recipes in the book were for brownies (moist and chocolatey) and fudge (meltingly sweet and addictive). I made my way through the book and usually met with success. The pages for apple crisp and chocolate frosting are very stained!

My only regret was that my mom refused to buy gumdrops so I could make Hidden Jewels: a brown-sugar bar filled with cut-up gumdrops. They're not as appealing to an adult palate, sadly—now that I can go to the grocery store and buy as many bags of gumdrops as I would ever want.

❧ Linda Davis Siess

❧

I grew up in a large, loud family of ten children on a farm in North Dakota. Between feeding her hungry brood and hired hands, my mom gave me the passion for learning and cooking.

I learned to cook from my mom by helping her. One of the things I remember is learning to peel apples for pie. We used to have contests to see who could peel the skin in the longest string. My mom always seemed to win until I learned the secret. *❧ Cynthia McConniel*

Cranberry Salad
Cynthia McConniel

12-oz. bag fresh cranberries, chopped
20-oz. can crushed pineapple, drained
10-oz. bag mini marshmallows
8-oz. container dairy whipped topping

1. Mix together the crushed pineapple and chopped cranberries.
2. Fold in whipped topping. Chill.
3. Just before serving, add marshmallows.

This salad is a quick, easy salad and a standard at all our holidays gatherings.

❦

When I was learning about nutrition in my eighth grade health class, the teacher asked us to keep a log of our meals for a week. The teacher was amazed at the variety of very nutritious food my mom prepared. She was thrilled.

My mom was a stickler—you could eat off her kitchen floor. So, I had lots of daily chores, which is not one of my favorite memories.

When I was in fourth grade, I told her I wanted to learn to cook like she did. She pointed me to the recipe books and said, "You can make whatever you want. All I ask is that the kitchen is as clean when you finish as it is right now." Then she disappeared for my entire foray into the culinary arts.

I fondly remember my first accomplishment: candle salad. A lettuce leaf base, pineapple ring on top of it, cottage cheese in the hole of the ring, half a peeled banana stuck into the cottage cheese, a split maraschino cherry on top for the flame, and some dribbled cherry juice down the banana for the final effect. I made that so often that I know my family grew to hate it.

❧ *Carol Lee*

I can remember like it was yesterday that the first thing that I made all by myself was toast with strawberry preserves. We didn't have a toaster, so it was toasted in the oven. My parents were out working in the yard, and I recall running the toast out to them. I was beaming! I was about 5 years old.

I remember one time when I was about 5 or 6. Mom had gotten me a miniature mixer. I used my Easy Bake Oven for a carrot cake and made the cream cheese frosting with my mixer.

If you happen to remember the Easy Bake Oven, those layers were paper thin. The frosting in between the layers was twice the size of the cakes! My brother didn't mind because cream cheese frosting with pecans was his favorite.

I still have that recipe for carrot cake that my grandmother wrote on a opened envelope. It's yellowed and has splatter marks on it, but it is framed and hanging in my kitchen. It's what I make for myself and for my kids on birthdays.

One time my mom agreed that I could cook the whole supper. I just knew I could handle it. As we say in the South, "Well, bless her heart!" The roast was tough, the gravy had scalded pieces in it, the macaroni was not cooked long enough, and I forgot to put the rolls out to rise.   ✿ *Angel Skelton*

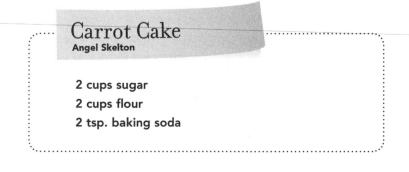

Carrot Cake
Angel Skelton

2 cups sugar

2 cups flour

2 tsp. baking soda

2 tsp. cinnamon

1¼ cup Wesson oil

4 eggs

3 cups grated carrots

Frosting:

½ cup (1 stick) butter, softened

8 oz. cream cheese, softened

1 lb. box powdered sugar

2½ tsp. vanilla

1 cup chopped pecans

2 Tbsp. warm milk, if needed

1. Stir dry ingredients together.
2. Add Wesson oil. Then add eggs, one at a time, beating after each one.
3. Last add grated carrots.
4. Bake in 2 or 3 layers (grease the pans) at 350° until toothpick inserted in middle comes out clean, 25-35 minutes.
5. Combine frosting ingredients except for pecans and milk. Mix well, adding milk if needed. Stir in pecans.
6. Spread between layers. Spread on top and sides.

❧

At age 12, I was beginning to bake recipes on my own. I followed one of my mother's recipes with her lefty, lousy handwriting and heated rather than beat the eggs. The cookies from that recipe *did not* turn out.

My sister always had her meals prepared by my mother and me. After she was married, she called me crying because she had no idea how to cook. We went to the grocery store together and had some great phone conversations for a few months afterwards as I taught her to cook via phone lines.

❧ *Tammy Johnson*

❧

My mom worked days when I was young, and my father worked evenings, so they didn't have to worry about childcare. In second grade when I was age 7, my mom would call me from work to talk me through cooking dinner for my dad.

The one thing I for sure remember making was salmon patties. I would stand on a chair at the counter with the phone with a really long cord while she talked me through each step. Mom was a secretary, and her co-workers got a kick out of listening to her. I even cooked those salmon patties myself, something we would never let a 7-year-old do today.

I remember canning beets from our garden when I was 12. It was a super hot Oklahoma day, and for once it was just my mom and me. My three brothers were off doing something (probably getting into trouble). I'll never forget the day or the pride I felt each time we opened a jar of those beets.

❧ *Gloria Schratwieser*

❧

I had to learn to cook early since my mother passed away when I was 5. My two German grandmothers raised me. I was forever standing beside them in the kitchen and learning everything they did. One of my grandmothers was almost pure German, so I learned how to make homemade cheese buttons and fried potatoes.

My other grandmother made lots of potluck dishes and

desserts because she was involved in the church so much, and there was always something to cook for. She made glorified rice a lot to take to get-togethers.

Since my dad was a farm hand with a local farmer, I tried to cook as much as possible so he could keep up his strength and feel satisfied. ❧ *Cindy Krous*

❧

When I got married, I could bake, but I couldn't really cook. I had helped a lot in the kitchen growing up, but Mama did the cooking. I think just watching and listening to Mama's explanations of what she was doing helped to launch me in my own kitchen.

I remember making my first salmon croquettes after I got married. They turned out great just because I could play the video in my head of Mama making them. ❧ *Diane Blaising*

Salmon Croquettes
Diane Blaising

1 big can (15 oz.) red salmon, bones, skin and all
2 eggs
12 saltine crackers
2 Tbsp. ketchup

1. Mix this up in a big bowl.
2. Divide into 8 portions. Shape each in a log shape and then pat it to make 3 long sides.
3. Roll each log in cornmeal.
4. Fry in a small amount of oil, over medium heat. Turn to a new side as each side gets crispy.
5. Serve with more ketchup.

※

My mom taught me to cook. Trained by George Perrier, chef at Le Bec Fin in Philadelphia, she cooked beautiful dishes every night and sang while she cooked. I was entranced by her singing and her cooking. I stood by her side from the age of 5, watching her exhibit skills and learning the fundamentals of sauces, cooking techniques, appropriate combinations, and inappropriate ones.   ❧ *Jeff Thal*

※

I can't remember not messing around in the kitchen. I'm sure my interest was kept alive because Mom would let us (my twin sister and me) lick the beaters and dip our fingers in the cookie dough. We even survived the raw dough!

Marlene Graber cherishes this picture because it is one of the earliest of her mom, Anna Miller Schrock. Anna was Amish until just before Marlene and her twin sister were born, and Amish culture discourages portraits. Here, Anna settles the twins (Darlene Schrock Hershey, left, and Marlene, right) for their 6-month photo in 1953 on the front lawn near Goshen, IN.

We sat on the countertop to watch her knead the bread or roll out the pie crusts. She'd pinch off small dough balls for us to use as our own. She had little bread pans and little pie tins for us to finish out our creations in the oven.

Any adventure I learned in the kitchen, though, was taught by my older sisters or in home ec class in high school, as Mom was a stick-by-the-tried-and-true kind of cook. I can't remember for sure what for flavoring or spice or process I wanted to add to a dish one time, but I do remember feeling frustrated that she didn't want to deviate!

"When I have my own kitchen...!" were my thoughts then, and I've done much experimenting since. But what I wouldn't give now to sit down to one of my mom's comforting "same old" meals.   ❧ *Marlene Graber*

Rivel Soup
Marlene Graber

1. Get about 2 quarts of milk to heating, with a pat of butter on top. In a bowl, preferably the bowl you plan to serve the soup in (to save on dirty dishes!), place about one generous cup of flour, one teaspoon salt, and in a hollow of flour, one egg Stir with a fork until you have irregular crumbs, about the size of shell beans. These are rivels.
2. Drop them, continually stirring, into the simmering milk, and cook for 5 minutes or so. The milk thickens slightly. Salt and pepper to taste. You can make more rivels in ratio to the milk, too, if you like.

There was always work to be done on our farm. There were two of us girls at the time, so one had to help Dad in the fields making fence or digging post holes, and the other worked in the house with Mom making pies. That was an easy decision: I chose to stay in.

When I was about 9 years old, Mom taught me to make my first pie and pie crust. Dad always liked to have a cake or pie for Sunday dinner, but pie was his favorite. I learned Crisco made good pie crusts, and the water in the recipe we used had to be ice cold.

My favorite book in Mom's cookbook collection was the *Farm Journal's Complete Pie Cookbook.* I tried lots of recipes. Some were delicious. I rated each recipe with either a smiley face or a frowny face. Very scientific. ❧ *Regina Martin*

When I was 13, Mom was hospitalized for massive blood clots. As was typical in the 1960s, Mom was the full-time homemaker, and Dad expected meat and potatoes when he arrived home from the office in the evening. My two older sisters had already moved out on their own, so the task fell to me.

I had never cooked anything before this time. Mom continued to decide the menu and called from the hospital telling me when to peel the potatoes, when to turn on the oven, etc. I made dinner each night for my dad and little sister. I learned to cook through telephone calls from my mother's hospital bed. ❧ *Karen Smith Christopherson*

I pulled up to the table with gusto every day when I was a kid. But I had zero interest in how the food got there.

I loved my little stove, sink, and fridge set, but that was clearly for pretend.

I got very whizzed up about making a real cake in my little kid oven when I was probably about eight. It was chocolate, it came out perfectly, and I wanted to make another one right away. But only a single box of mix had come with the oven. I could not figure out how wet batter turned into dry crumbs.

I was totally charmed by my *Betty Crocker's Cook Book for Boys and Girls*. I must have looked at it a lot, because when I flip through it now, I remember lots of the drawings, photos, and recipe names. But I only ever made Eggs in a

Phyllis Pellman Good, age 3 or 4, swiping a taste of the just-baked pie before everyone else had arrived at the table.

Frame on page 66! How did this happen? We didn't have TV, so I guess I had too many good books to read.

That was the extent of my cooking experience when Merle volunteered to clean—and I said I'd cook—after we got married! ❧ *Phyllis Pellman Good*

❧

I actually learned to cook from my grandma back in the '40s. She was widowed at a young age, and my mom was a single mom at a young age, so it only seemed natural that we all lived together in Grandma's big house. Mom worked fulltime, and Grandma ran the house including cooking and baking—not only for the four of us, but for the scores of relatives who seemed to love to come stay for a while.

Grandma was one of those wonderful Depression-era cooks who never threw anything out and could make an interesting feast out of whatever she had on hand, especially leftovers. She made everything from scratch. There were no instant mixes back then.

I don't remember her *ever* making something we didn't enjoy—maybe because we all adored her. There were cherry trees and black walnut trees in our yard. It was lots of work for us kids to pick and clean them, but we got to devour the rewards, of course.

The most amazing thing is that Grandma did not own nor write down recipes! Not a cookbook in the house! How did she throw together wonderful meals and amazing desserts out of her head? As I grew older, I realized that's why nothing was ever the same twice. She used whatever she had on hand—a confident cook out of necessity.   ✖ *Diane Doyle*

✖

I remember trying to make a cake for dessert as a surprise for Mom. I wasn't very experienced in the kitchen and didn't know the difference between confectioners sugar and granulated sugar. When it came time to frost the cake, I made the wrong choice. Everyone graciously tried to eat it, but it was like eating sand. We still have lots of laughs at my first attempt to make a cake all by myself.

✖ *Becky McClees*

Chocolate Mint Sails

Becky McClees
Makes 2 dozen

Brownies:
½ cup (1 stick) butter
1 cup sugar
1 tsp. vanilla
2 eggs
2 1-oz. squares unsweetened chocolate, melted
½ cup flour
½ cup chopped walnuts

Frosting:
1 cup powdered sugar
3 Tbsp. butter, divided
1 Tbsp. light cream
½ tsp. peppermint extract
green food coloring
1-oz. square unsweetened chocolate
1 Tbsp. butter

1. Cream butter, sugar, and vanilla.
2. Add eggs, beating well. Blend in chocolate, then add flour and nuts.
3. Bake in a greased 8x8x2 pan at 350° for 25-30 minutes. Cool.
4. For frosting, combine sugar, 2 Tbsp. butter, cream, peppermint, and green coloring; beat well.
5. Spread over cooled brownie layer; let stand till set.
6. Melt together chocolate and remaining 1 Tbsp. butter. Drizzle melted chocolate mixture over frosting.
7. Chill until firm. Cut in triangles. Serve up on edge like sails.

꤮

I grew up in rural Maine on a family-run farm. My earliest experience that I can clearly remember is from when I was 5 years old. My mom was pregnant and having a terrible pregnancy. I made my brother's lunches for school during this time.

My grammie would put a casserole or a pot roast together and bring it to our house. At the time she had told me, I would put it in the oven. It was always planned to be done when my dad got home from the barn, so my brother and I wouldn't be handling anything right out of the oven. I was always so proud, as though I had made it all myself! It wasn't long before I could.   ✿ *Jean Crowell*

꤮

I had to grow up fast due to the fact that many times my mother was unable to cook because she had cancer and was too sick. I had some help from all my claimed grandparents—most from the neighborhood and some from our little country church.

After she had her breast removed, the doctors told Mom that she wouldn't be able to use her arms like she used to because of how they had to go in and remove the cancer. They didn't know my mom! She learned to make bread to get her arms working again!

By the time I was 12, I could make just about anything I wanted: meatloaf, gravy, biscuits, breads, pies, cakes, you name it. Even though it was something I was forced to do, and it made my mom feel bad at the time, I am so thankful because I wouldn't be the person I am today. I know my mom's watching over me and smiling.   ✿ *Marie Anderson*

My name is Kirsten, and I'm 10 years old. My mom is the best baker in the world. One of her favorite things to bake is peanut butter cup cookies. I always help her by unwrapping hundreds and hundreds of the little Reese's peanut butter cups.

One of the things that makes this fun is that whenever she says, "Surprise," I am allowed to eat one of the little peanut butter cups that I've unwrapped. Another thing is that I'm being a help to her.

As I'm getting older, she is letting me help her do the actual baking now. That's even more fun! ✒ *Kirsten Dreps*

Little Cheddar Loaves
Kirsten Dreps

1 egg
¾ cup milk
1 cup shredded cheese
½ cup quick oats
1 tsp. salt
1 lb. ground beef
⅔ cup ketchup
½ cup brown sugar
1½ tsp. mustard

1. Beat egg and milk. Stir in cheese and oats and salt. Add beef and mix.
2. Shape into little loaves. Place in a baking dish.
3. Combine ketchup, brown sugar and mustard and mix. Spoon over loaves.
4. Bake uncovered at 350° for 45 minutes or so.

In 1978 when I was 9, we moved to northern Idaho where we built a house out in the woods without electricity or running water. We had to learn how to cook using a wood-burning stove and oven. Cooking became a family event and challenge. That is where I learned how to use a pressure cooker, which I still use to this day.

My parents taught me how to make homemade apple pie, with a crust from scratch, and lasagna—all using the wood-burning oven. Waffles were homemade and cooked in a cast iron waffle maker on top of the stove.

Imagine how happy I was when I married my husband and found out that their hunting camp had a wood-burning oven. I surprised them by making lasagna and apple pie when they were out hunting one day. No one in recent years had used the oven.

My family had a very cold winter the first year in Idaho, and there were a lot of days we didn't go to school. My mom didn't work, so the day was spent cooking and hauling wood. It was a very rough winter, but we stood hard as a family.

We didn't have electricity, so there was no TV. We read together, played board games, and went cross-country skiing. It was a pretty magical time for me as a 9 year old.

I think the biggest thing my parents taught me about cooking is patience. Things don't always come out the way you intended, but you keep trying. And to this day I still think that food cooked in a wood-burning oven is the best.

❧ *Carol Spencer*

I was always interested in cooking as a child, and many times I helped my mom with traditional holiday foods. Her specialties were lasagna and rice stuffing.

For helping her, I always got a bowl of rice stuffing when we were done making it. To this day I make her rice stuffing and eat a bowl when I'm done.   *Claire Van Cott*

Mom's Rice and Chopmeat Stuffing
Claire Van Cott

1 large onion, chopped
½ cup (one stick) butter, *divided*
3 ribs celery with leaves, chopped
16 oz. white mushrooms, sliced
1½ lbs. ground beef (chopmeat)
1 Tbsp. oil, *optional*
3 hardboiled eggs, peeled and
   chopped
1 cup raisins
½ lb. long grain white rice,
   cooked
kosher salt
pepper

My mom use to boil and chop up the turkey giblets and add them to the stuffing. I don't do this part and the stuffing is still delish.

I love, love, love this stuffing. It's a family favorite.

1. Saute onion in ½ stick butter. Set aside.
2. Saute celery and mushrooms in the other ½ stick butter.
3. Brown ground beef, using a tbsp. of oil if necessary.
4. In a large bowl, combine sauteed veggies, ground beef, eggs, raisins, and rice. Add salt and pepper to taste.

5. Put mixture in greased oven-proof dish and bake at 350° for 20-40 minutes, until warmed through. I sometimes dot the top with a little butter—not too much! You can also stuff a turkey with this stuffing. The juices from the turkey make it taste even better.

༄

Today at 91 years of age my memories of childhood come easily. Shadowing my mother around the house, I accepted small chores and mimicked her ways. Hulling peas, snapping beans, and husking fresh corn did not seem like work.

When it was time to make pies, she always made several and gave me the dough scraps to make my very own three-inch pie. I felt so accomplished one time when she had me prepare a simple recipe and serve it to my school friends.

Another cherished memory is of Mother and me at the kitchen sink. She would wash and sing hymns by memory, and I would dry. Our kitchen had modern appliances but no radio.

How did Mother become so capable in the kitchen?

Barbara Ebersole Brubaker, Naomi's mother, holding her first grandchild, Catherine Fast, in her flower garden on Rose Ave. in Lancaster, PA in 1951.

Although her schooling had ended at sixth grade, her curious nature helped her to self-educate herself from many sources. Magazines such as *Good Housekeeping* and *Better Homes and Gardens* came by mail monthly. I remember her clipping recipes and preparing them—to open up our taste buds.

She had several cookbooks, including a first edition of the *Mennonite Community Cookbook* by Mary Emma Show-alter—now owned by my daughter. In this cookbook, there are yellowed newspaper clippings for roast lamb Syrian style and scalloped salmon divan as well as Mother's handwritten recipe for Shrewsbury cookies. What a treasure!

In 1943 when I graduated from Goshen College with a degree in home economics, I felt that my mother deserved equal honor. During my high school and college years, she would read and discuss my textbooks with me. She became my mentor and could have received her own degree.

🍃 *Naomi Brubaker Fast*

🌿

We had a bar that overlooked the stove top and divided the family room from the kitchen. The smells of Mom preparing food always drew me to one of those barstools as she cooked—assuming my homework was done, of course. There we would debrief my day as she prepared the meal that was generating all those wonderful smells.

We didn't have a lot of money, so Mom made her own version of dishes we'd otherwise only heard about. One was what we called beef stroganoff, but it bore little resemblance to the dish I finally saw in a restaurant.

Mom's beef stroganoff had tomato soup as its base with some Worcestershire sauce and sour cream mixed in with a few seasonings and a bay leaf or two—all simmered together with ground beef and served over rice. I've repeatedly tried to reproduce Mom's recipe, and my children, who don't know any different, really like it. But I know I'm still a ways off of Mom's version.

But this won't be complete until I tell you about the pancakes. My dad made us pancakes every Saturday morning, and each time he would experiment with a different ingredient—from corn (which is really quite good) to applesauce (also good) to Hawaiian Punch (it took a great effort to get over the pink pancakes and the fruity taste).

When I was old enough, Dad turned his spatula over to me. Today, I carry his tradition forward in our house.

❧ *David Fry*

I was 3 years old. It was a cold Virginia morning on the day after Halloween, and my mother was cooking down the pumpkin from our jack-o-lanterns. The kitchen was warm with the smells of spices and pumpkin.

Mom pulled a stool up to the counter for me and gave me a potato masher to smash the cooked, cooled pumpkin. We talked about everything we were doing and why. Mom had me count as she measured the sugar, eggs, and cream. She added the spices and let me stir it all up. We poured the mixture into pie crusts and froze them for the upcoming holidays.

When the pies were later baked and served, Mom told everyone how I had helped. I was so very proud, and I think my love of cooking was born from this special time with my mother. To this day when I smell pumpkin pie spices, it takes me right back to that morning with my mom.

❧ *Donika Engstrom*

My mother's mother died when Mom was only 13, so she had to drop out of school to care for her younger brother who was only about 8 years old at the time. She didn't know how to cook much, but some neighbor ladies helped her, and over the years, she became a very good cook.

My mom learned to make pie crust later in life. My dad's mom gave her a recipe for pie crust, which Grandma said was foolproof. Mom practiced and became an excellent pie baker.

I started cooking in elementary school, but I really took

Extra-Tender Pastry
Rebecca Loach

2 cups flour
¼ tsp. salt
½ cup shortening
1 egg, beaten
1 Tbsp. cider vinegar
3 Tbsp. water

1. Stir together flour and salt. Cut in shortening until pieces are the size of small peas.
2. In a small bowl, blend together the egg, vinegar, and water.
3. Add a few spoonfuls of the flour mixture to the egg mixture to form a paste.
4. Add the paste to the rest of the flour mixture. Press into a ball shape. Divide in half and form into two disk shapes.
5. Wrap each disk individually with plastic wrap and refrigerate for at least twenty minutes. (This step is important and really helps to make the dough easier to work with by fully hydrating the flour.)
6. Roll out dough and fit into pie pans.

off in my culinary exploits after a course in home economics in seventh grade. Since Mom had started cooking so early in life, she was glad to have some help in the kitchen.

I started baking in earnest in eighth grade after visiting a cousin who baked all her breads using something called Spruance bread mix. It came in a five-pound bag and contained a little foil packet of yeast. All you had to add was water, and you could make four loaves of bread. Mom had never baked with yeast, so this was a new adventure in our kitchen.

🌿 *Rebecca Loach*

M other would hold our hands and guide the whisking of muffin batter or the handle of a soup ladle. She tolerated spills and burnt food so we could learn.

Mother never used a cookbook and rarely referred to a recipe. If she didn't know what to make for supper, she would always start with an onion. It was just like magic to us children, because after a while, out would come a soup or a casserole or some unnameable dish that varied in style, taste, or culture. People have teased mother that she should write her own cookbook called *God, Mama, and an Onion.*

Mother also never measured anything. She'd eyeball and guess until it was just right. It sure was frustrating to us when we'd follow directions with cooking and try to copy Mother's instructions. But now I laugh to myself when I do that very thing. Those habits have tagged along with me to my own home, and now I'm teaching the next generation how to improvise.

🌿 *Sara Meyers*

When I was in the fifth grade and 12 years old, the girls in my class were supposed to make a complete meal for our classroom. Three of us twelve girls were responsible to make meatloaf, so Mom taught me all the ins and outs of it to make sure it would be good.

It was a hit with my classmates, and from then on, Mom often had me make meatloaf for our family. ❧ *Naomi Cross*

Naomi Cross celebrating her eleventh birthday with school friends. It was a rare treat, friends overnight.

❧

Looking back, it seems I've known how to cook for a long, long time with no clear memories of a first time. Mom started my sisters and me with dish washing.

When I was around 3 years old, she pulled a chair to the kitchen sink and let me scrub to my heart's delight. I liked to get the burned-on food scoured from the pots and pans. Oh, the satisfaction of a shining clean surface!

Mom always says you have to let children help when they are interested so they will want to help when they are old enough. So we were at her elbow licking spoons or beaters, and as we got older and stronger, stirring ingredients or learning to run the electric mixer.

She was good at getting us involved even though I am sure it lengthened her kitchen time. Her first love is being outside with all her beautiful flowers.

Gradually we girls took on a lot of food preparation. Our family doctor arrived at the house to check on Mom after our youngest sister was born. He was astounded to see my 10-year-old sister and me busily cooking supper for the family. To us it wasn't a unique occurrence, and we still chuckle about his astonishment. ✿ *Becky S. Frey*

Kitchen Comedy

My mother taught home ec at our local high school. Late one night when I was in high school, she remembered that the principal had asked her to make cookies for the teachers' meeting the next day. She sent me to the store to see if I could find anything that would be easy and fast as it was almost 9 p.m. when she remembered.

Pre-made cookie dough seemed the best thing to get. When I got home, I made the cookies and decorated them for my mom. The next day I had teachers telling me how delicious the cookies were. Several of them asked for the recipe. All I could do was say, " Oh, the recipe is a family secret," so they wouldn't know the home ec teacher didn't make them from scratch! ❧ *Joanne Maynard*

My mom was lots of fun growing up, but she could not cook. I taught myself to cook out of self-preservation.

One time she made some bread and set it on the counter to cool. Our dog jumped up and took it off the counter and buried it in the backyard.

Another time I had a slumber party, and she was making us pancakes in the morning. She tried to do a fancy flip and flipped the pancakes right into the ceiling fan. They splattered all over the room.

One time she made me fried eggs that were so rubbery that the dog wouldn't eat them. I tried to put them down the garbage disposal, and they literally popped back out into the sink. Bless her heart. But we sure had fun. And I sure can cook now! ❧ *Gretchen*

❧

I am the youngest of four children. By the time I came along, children were not welcome in my mother's kitchen. She was a great cook, and she just didn't like little hands in her kitchen.

When I was 8 years old, Mom graduated from the LVN program and worked the graveyard shift for the rest of her career.

She was determined that this would not affect her "housewifely" duties and, trust me, it didn't. I turned 18 and still thought the clothes fairy came and picked up my clothes from off the floor, washed them, dried them, ironed them, and hung them in my closet.

She had one concession to her full schedule. She would come home from work in the morning and, after doing the laundry, the floors, and the dusting, would make a casserole and leave my older brother and me directions about how to heat it for dinner.

We had a gas stove. In order to light the oven, we had to turn on the gas and then, with a match, light the pilot light. My brother and I would turn on the gas and then proceed to let it run while we argued over who had to endanger life and limb to light the pilot light. I don't know why it never occurred to us that if we just did it, our eyebrows and my bangs would not be in danger.

I spent most of my tenth year with singed eyebrows, and I still don't like casseroles.   ❧ *Sandy Swopes*

❧

It was my job to clear the table after dinner. I was about 7 when it dawned on me that the ice cube families in my iced tea glass met with a tragic death under the scalding hot water in the sink. So I started rescuing them. After every meal, I stuffed them in the back of the freezer.

For months this went on until Mom ran out of room in the freezer and discovered what caused it. I got spanked. She had my brother clear the table and gave me his job of taking scraps to the back fencerow.

I met a really nice stray cat there. I started feeding her closer and closer to the back door until I had us a cat. And she did the right thing to pay us back: she had seven kittens. I remember rolling balls down the hallway and twenty-eight kitten feet pounding after them on the pine floors—pure joy and fits of laughter.

My mom would say thirty years later, after many cats had stolen her heart and warmed her feet and romped down that

My mom was always fixing food and forgetting it. Subsequently, she was taken out to dinner frequently and her kitchen was spotless.

hallway, that perhaps she'd been a bit hasty to spank me over the ice cubes. ✿ *Lori Fleming Browne*

We had just moved when I was 14, and a family member gave us a bag of groceries. Mom was teaching me how to make Spanish rice.

I poured some oil in the pan and noticed that the rice looked funny. Mom said it was fine, so I poured the rice into the hot pan, and it started to pop. The rice was mostly maggots! I screamed, and Mom screamed, and Dad saved us by throwing it all out. ✿ *Lucy Craig*

When I was 10 years old, my mom made Thanksgiving dinner for a few friends and a young couple who rented our cabin. Right before it was time to eat, we heard my mom in the kitchen say, "Oh my gosh!"

We all went in to see what was wrong, and she was saying, "Look! The turkey shrank! I'll never be able to feed all these people with this little turkey!" It was only about six inches long.

After a few minutes of everyone being in shock and trying to help Mom figure out what to do, she burst into laughter and brought out the real twenty-pound turkey. She had switched in a Cornish game hen as a joke on us.

✿ *Marci McGarvey*

Dad had been fishing. He brought his catch back and left them in the kitchen sink to clean later. My brother and I, who were in early grade school, decided we would help. We pulled a kitchen chair up to the sink and proceeded to clean the fish with Johnson's baby shampoo, so we "wouldn't hurt their eyes."

Mom caught us in the act and hurried to grab the camera to take some photos before she told Dad. Dad buried the squeaky-clean mess of trout, and Mom had some gorgeous roses that summer. ✺ *Debbie Browning*

One day when I was in third grade or so, I came home to the wonderful aroma of Mom's raisin fried pies. I was so disappointed to have to wait until after supper to have one.

After one bite, Dad spit his right back out on the plate! My brothers and I were soon gagging as well. Mom had tears in her eyes—what had gone wrong? The pies were totally inedible.

My 4-year-old brother was soon found to be the culprit. He was constantly sneaking into the sugar and eating it by the handful. This time, to cover his tracks, he had poured the entire box of salt into the sugar canister! ✺ *Tammy Coder*

We lived on a lake, and my grandparents and parents went fishing before lunch one time. I went into the kitchen and saw an empty pie plate on the floor, so I picked it up and put it in the sink to be washed.

When they got back to eat lunch, Grandma looked around and asked where the pie was that she fixed. I wondered if the empty pie plate in the sink had something to do with it, and Grandma accused me of eating it. I said, "No way, it was empty on the floor." And then we looked at our dog, Rocket, and he looked so guilty!

To this day we don't know how that dog got the pie in its glass plate off the counter and onto the tile floor without breaking it. We did laugh about it, but until her death, Grandma always talked about that darn dog who ate her pie!

          ❧ *Cindy Bertoncin*

Phyllis is held by her mother, Betty Pellman, on Christmas Day in 1949, while enjoying one of many gifts that day.

We were a dog family. The dog lived outside, of course. My mom was a no-dog-hair-in-the-house person.

Then one day, somebody gave us a kitten. My brother and I were charmed. My mom was not. But somehow the kitten was allowed to stay in the house, despite Ma's clearly stated suspicions—"Cats are sneaky. They're too quiet. You never know what they're doing."

Turns out she was right.

We were having guests for dinner one evening, and Ma had baked a chocolate cake. It was sitting on the counter cooling, waiting to be iced. There must have been a moment when we were all out of the kitchen. What I am clear about was Ma's shriek. "Look at this," she hollered.

There, on the soft, spongy top of the cooling cake was a path of paw prints. Our sweet little kitten had taken a stroll across the cake.

That was one of the last days our cat spent with us before it moved on to a new home.   *Phyllis Pellman Good*

❧

One day around suppertime, a family friend dropped by with some paperwork for my dad. We kids were all hanging around the kitchen, probably trolling for a snack before dinner (not allowed) and happy to chat with Mr. F. instead of attacking our homework.

Supper that night was going to star my mom's homemade corn chowder, a buttery, milky broth with potatoes, onions, and corn, salt and pepper—rich and satisfying on a chilly day.

Mr. F. commented on the kettle of chowder bubbling away on the stovetop, and my mom offered him a bowlful. We kids ("We're starving!") were not offered any, because it wasn't suppertime. So we watched Mr. F. take a spoonful, chew thoughtfully, and swallow slowly, with a strange look on his face. My mother, horrified, asked what was wrong.

"Oh, nothing at all," said Mr. F. "The potatoes are just a little...ah...chewy." He took another spoonful and chewed manfully and swallowed. "But that's just the way I like them!"

He really didn't fool anybody. Who likes undercooked potatoes? But he was a great gentleman and taught us kids a lesson in politeness that day.

Of course, every single time my mother ever made chowder again, one or another of us smart-aleck kids would ask, "Say, Mom, are you sure the potatoes are cooked?" And my mom would reply, pretending to be mad, "Stop it! Of the millions of meals I've made for you, that's the only thing you can remember?" 	**>** *Linda Davis Siess*

>><

I don't know the origin of this recipe. I just know that my mother-in-law made it and loved teasing people that it really was Ritz crackers even though no one believed her! Her sense of humor and teasing was loved by all.

> *Carol Findling*

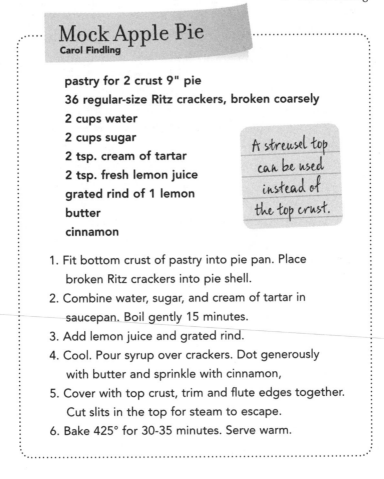

Mock Apple Pie
Carol Findling

pastry for 2 crust 9" pie
36 regular-size Ritz crackers, broken coarsely
2 cups water
2 cups sugar
2 tsp. cream of tartar
2 tsp. fresh lemon juice
grated rind of 1 lemon
butter
cinnamon

A streusel top can be used instead of the top crust.

1. Fit bottom crust of pastry into pie pan. Place broken Ritz crackers into pie shell.
2. Combine water, sugar, and cream of tartar in saucepan. Boil gently 15 minutes.
3. Add lemon juice and grated rind.
4. Cool. Pour syrup over crackers. Dot generously with butter and sprinkle with cinnamon,
5. Cover with top crust, trim and flute edges together. Cut slits in the top for steam to escape.
6. Bake 425° for 30-35 minutes. Serve warm.

There is one incident, which is a good word for it, that happened when I was probably about 10 years old. My neighbor friend and I decided to make oatmeal cookies. My mother asked if she could help, but we said, "No, we can read the instructions."

When we saw oatmeal in the recipe, we cooked it in the tall kettle that was normally used as a double boiler. We mixed up everything in the recipe, including the cooked oatmeal, and baked the most delicious cookies—delicious only while they were warm, however. After that they could have been used as hockey pucks! ❧ *Carol Findling*

❧

When I was growing up, we were very lucky to have my grandmother, Bop (Polish for "grandmother"), live with us. She was an immigrant from Poland—short, round, and tough as nails. She loved to cook because she *loved* seeing people eat her food.

I was a fussy eater, but French fries were always my favorite. Every day she would hand cut her home grown potatoes, scrape yesterday's shortening from a coffee can, and fry up a batch of crispy home fries for me. (How I don't weigh 300 pounds, I'll never know.) To remove some of the grease from the fries, she would always take a recycled paper grocery bag and shake the fries in it.

One day, I sat with my heaping plate of fries before me, squeezing out ketchup over them, and sprinkling them with white vinegar. I was ready to indulge. Just before I took my first bite, I spotted a hair, which I quietly, quickly removed. Not discouraged, I lifted a fry, but there was another hair, and another, and another.

It was then I realized that Bop had used the paper bag that the cat had played in the night before. The story is retold year after year, and we still get a good laugh from it.

        🦋 *Joanne Kennedy*

🦋

My older brother was a newlywed. His new wife, Vicky, was in the kitchen with my mom. She was very nervous to make a good impression.

In the process of cooking, my mom turned suddenly with a butcher knife in her hand and accidentally poked Vicky. We still tease my mom about the time she stabbed Vicky, but Vicky didn't even have a nick on her, and she grew very close with the whole family.

        🦋 *Gloria Schratwieser*

🦋

My twin sister and I freely enjoyed interacting with our older sisters' boyfriends, as we were a good ten or so years younger than they were. (We *may* have pestered them as well.) There was one funny accident I remember that we didn't let one of the suitors forget for a long time.

When he came into the house, he was thirsty. He raided the fridge and spied a glass of what he thought was lemonade. He took a big swig of it and could hardly get it out of his mouth fast enough! It was egg whites that my mom had saved from making noodles with the yolks!

He laughed right along with us. I don't exactly remember, but that may have been the weekend that he proposed to my sister.

        🦋 *Marlene Graber*

❦

One day Mom was in the kitchen chopping celery to put in potato soup for lunch. My cousin Jim was there, and he was going to eat lunch with us. He wanted to know what Aunt Gladys was fixing.

Before Mom had a chance to answer, I said, "Potato soup." Jim said, "I don't like potato soup."

Mom spoke up and said, "It's not potato soup. It's celery soup."

Jim ate two bowls and thought it was delicious. I was so proud of my mom. I didn't know she could think so fast!

❦ *Barbara Land*

❦

I remember the year my dad decided it could be a man's job to cook the Thanksgiving turkey at our home using our newest gadget—a big metal box called a microwave. This thing came with a probe.

My mom was home and prepared to be impressed by the effort. I was 9 years old and cautiously curious to see this spectacle. Dad brined, seasoned, and stuffed the turkey. He placed the probe in the bird's breast near the the leg and programmed the musical keys. He pushed the start button and walked away.

I was the only one to see that bird start to move. I shrieked when a bright spark flew. There was a big bang! The turkey had busted through the ceiling of the microwave, destroying it.

The turkeys of yesteryear came with a metal truss for the legs. I guess Dad skipped that part when he read the instructions. We had Chinese that year! ❦ *Sherry B. Carrier*

❧

Despite her clean and tidy ways, my mother was quite indulgent about letting us kids experiment in her sparkling kitchen. One day after school, my friend Sharon and I decided to make a strawberry Quik cake from a recipe on the back of a container of strawberry milk mix.

We made the recipe all right and *ate the entire cake ourselves.* That night, I was so ill. My mother didn't scold or reprimand me. I think she knew I had been punished sufficiently. To this day, I flinch when I see strawberry milk in the store.

❦ *Kate Silverstein*

❧

When I got home from school, my step-mom would call from work and give me some directions for supper preparations. Once, when I was 15, she called and told me to get out six potatoes and prick each one with a fork and put them in the oven at 350 until she got home.

I got out six potatoes and six forks. I put a fork in each potato and put them in the oven to bake. My younger sister asked me why the forks were in the potatoes. I told her it must have something to do with the baking. Just to make sure, I called Mom back at work and said, "Mom, you told me to get out six potatoes and prick each one with a fork and leave them in the 350 oven until you get home, right?"

She said, "Yes that is correct." Well, she was very surprised when she came home and saw the baked forks and potatoes.

❦ *Donna Spencer*

❧

I would love to go back to our home in 1969 to eat dinner with my family, in the same kitchen, at the same table. I would eat those Brussel sprouts that I hid in the hollow table leg. I would take back the lie I told my mother when she asked if I ate them. Then she wouldn't have had to clean the whole kitchen looking for where that awful smell was coming from. ❧ *Toni Thoma*

When he was a teenager, my oldest brother woke up to a strange and obnoxious burning smell. His nose led him to the kitchen stove where Mom had started cooking rhubarb before bed and forgot it.

When he lifted the lid, there was a glowing glob in the bottom of the pot and unbelievable smoke. He took care of the mess, but the consequence was that the smoke caused him to become sleepless.

He got in our vehicle and drove around until daybreak. He later found out that Native Americans smoked rhubarb as a natural stimulant. ❧ *Rebecca Meyerkorth*

Treats

When I was in grammar school, I told my mother that I wanted to have a school friend come over after school—so please remember.

When we came in after school, the house was so nice and smelled like homemade oatmeal cookies. My mother had set the kitchen table for us using her best china. She had flowers in her china teapot. We had hot dogs and potato chips.

The house was spotless.

My uncle who usually got all the special privileges had to let us watch TV that day, and Mom even made him go outside to smoke his cigars. She made me feel like a princess for an afternoon.

The next day we reversed, and I went to my friend's house after school. Her mom was at work, so my friend and her brother were latchkey children. It seemed like a toy store in the brother's room, and my friend had ever so many dolls.

The house seemed a mansion compared to our small home, but it was in disarray.

We found a package of store-bought cookies but no milk in the house. I began to feel like I was the richest little girl in the world and couldn't wait to get back to my mom and our comfy little home. 🍂 *Ann Scroggins Lucas*

We normally didn't have birthday parties with friends to celebrate our birthdays. We just had a special time with family. But when I was 9 years old, I had a birthday party at my house. I asked Mama to make her chocolate pie for me instead of a birthday cake.

I had nine girls at the party around the table, and we had chocolate pie with candles in the meringue and chocolate ice cream, too. My friends thought it was a little weird to have pie and not cake, but no one complained because Mama's chocolate pie was a big hit. I make her chocolate pie every Thanksgiving and Christmas and remember my ninth birthday. 🍂 *Diane Blaising*

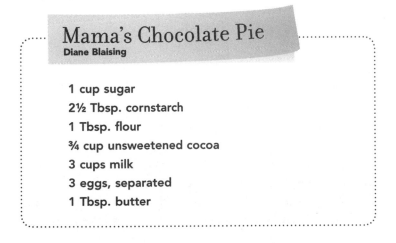

Mama's Chocolate Pie
Diane Blaising

1 cup sugar
2½ Tbsp. cornstarch
1 Tbsp. flour
¾ cup unsweetened cocoa
3 cups milk
3 eggs, separated
1 Tbsp. butter

1½ tsp. vanilla
9" baked pie shell

1. Cook sugar, cornstach, flour, cocoa, and milk in saucepan and boil 1 minute, stirring.
2. Add a little of the hot mixture to the egg yolks, stirring, and then add the mixture back to the saucepan. Boil another minute, stirring.
3. Take off the heat and add butter and vanilla. Set aside to cool slightly and whip the egg whites until stiff to make meringue.
4. Pour chocolate mixture in baked pie shell. Top with meringue and slightly brown in 400° oven.

❧

When I was a little girl, my mom would wash my hair at bath time. She would tell me to look up to keep the shampoo out of my eyes and to look for the pink elephants. So for my eighth birthday, she made me a pink elephant cake. My childhood was amazing! ❧ *Holley Rashott*

❧

We were all sitting around the supper table one evening waiting for dessert. Mother had made a homemade apple pie, which was a real treat that we didn't get very often.

She had put it out to cool, but when she went to get it, it was gone. We looked everywhere, but we didn't find it. About a week later the pie plate reappeared, but we never did find out what exactly had happened. ❧ *Howard Higgins*

I searched for a long time for Grandma Renata's cookie recipe because my husband had asked me to make them for a long time. Her cookbooks were all written in German, and we kept none of them—much to our sorrow.

In 2008, I found this recipe on a website for "forgotten recipes." I am hoping that this is the recipe that Grandma Renata used. My husband says they are darn close!

🍃 *Carol Findling*

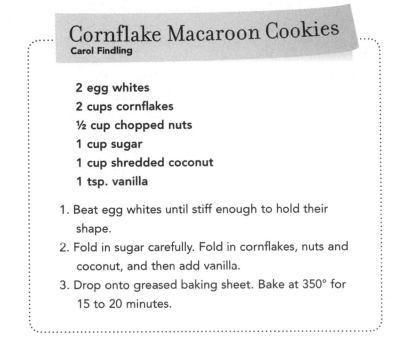

Cornflake Macaroon Cookies
Carol Findling

2 egg whites
2 cups cornflakes
½ cup chopped nuts
1 cup sugar
1 cup shredded coconut
1 tsp. vanilla

1. Beat egg whites until stiff enough to hold their shape.
2. Fold in sugar carefully. Fold in cornflakes, nuts and coconut, and then add vanilla.
3. Drop onto greased baking sheet. Bake at 350° for 15 to 20 minutes.

One year, my mom told me she didn't have time to bake a cake for my birthday. I was very hurt but tried not to show it because she worked so hard every day. Farming in the '60s wasn't easy.

When supper was over and the dishes cleared away, she asked me to go into the other room to get her something, likely yarn for one of the many projects she would work on to relax in the evenings. I was so surprised to find a beautiful doll cake that she had made and decorated for me on my birthday, April 1—April Fool's Day. It was the best cake ever!

🌿 *Dianne Lane*

🌿

My mother was a Christmas fanatic. The house was completely decorated, outside and inside, every single room. In our culture, we celebrate Las Posadas, the journey of Mary and Joseph searching for an inn in preparation for the birth of Jesus. It's quite an event with praying, singing, laughter, and food. We always expected many guests, even in bad weather.

My mother's claim to fame was that she fed everyone very well as those parties. Most of our friends would serve cookies, punch, or hot chocolate. My mother would have elaborate meals that included her famous tamales.

She taught me to make tamales in the winter of 1980. She said I was old enough to learn. It's a laborious process with many steps, and she was anxious for me to learn so I could help her for years to come. We prepared the masa, spread the masa on the corn husks, prepared the filling, and filled each tamale while she told me stories about how her mother taught her and her mother's mother taught her.

I knew I had arrived as a young lady. It was a rite of passage for her to teach me. Not everyone makes tamales, she explained. "It's all in the hands." She hoped that someday I would teach my children to make them and the tradition would continue.

🌿 *Maria Garcia*

W hen I was a little girl, my favorite snack was popcorn. In the evening after homework was done and I had taken my bath and put on my pajamas, my mom and I would make popcorn the old-fashioned way on the stove in a pan.

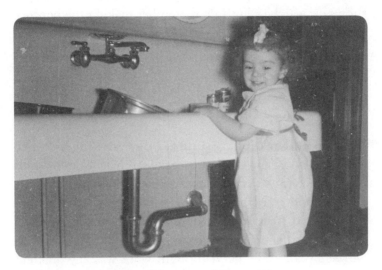

Rose C. Speicher doing dishes as a toddler in 1958.

Mom would get out the six-quart stainless pan and cover the bottom of the pan with vegetable oil and set it on the electric burner to heat. We had one of those red step stools that were common in the fifties, and I would stand on the step watching her.

As soon as the first kernel popped, she would add the rest of the popcorn and quickly put the lid on the pan. Like magic, we would hear the kernels begin to pop, first slowly then speeding up rapidly, sounding like fireworks on the Fourth of July!

As soon as the popping slowed again, Mom would take

the pan off the stove to reveal a huge pan full of tender, hot, white popcorn that immediately went into a big yellow ceramic bowl that we called the popcorn bowl.

Mom would then melt some butter in the hot pan and pour it over the freshly popped corn, finishing it off with a shake or two of salt. We would take the bowl of popcorn into the living room and watch TV.

The funny thing is that I don't remember many of the shows we watched, but I do remember making the popcorn and cuddling on the sofa with Mom while we shared that sacred bowl of popcorn.   ✿ *Rose C. Speicher*

I would go back to any summer day growing up when we would vacuum the house, make sandwiches, and pack a picnic lunch to go to the beach for a couple of hours and read.

My mother, Mary, was very good about making work pleasant and recognizing that you need to mix life up with fun too. Our family led a very simple life, but I never knew we were poor, and I never thought work was any different than play.   ✿ *Ruthe Ploskunyak*

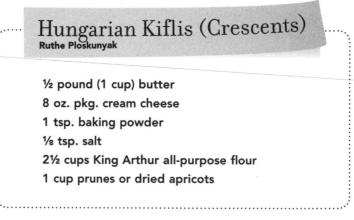

Hungarian Kiflis (Crescents)
Ruthe Ploskunyak

½ pound (1 cup) butter

8 oz. pkg. cream cheese

1 tsp. baking powder

⅛ tsp. salt

2½ cups King Arthur all-purpose flour

1 cup prunes or dried apricots

½ **cup water**
confectioners sugar

1. Beat together the cream cheese and butter. Stir in the baking powder, salt, and flour. Refrigerate.
2. While dough is chilling, make filling. Boil fruit in water in open pan until soft. Puree with a blender or immersion blender. Set aside to cool.
3. Roll dough out thin. Cut into 2-½" squares.
4. Fill with about 1 tsp. of filling. (Leftover filling can be frozen). Fold over one corner into the middle, moisten it, and then fold the opposite corner over it and seal.
5. Bake at 350° for 20-22 minutes on parchment lined sheets.
6. After the crescents are baked and just before serving, sprinkle with confectioners sugar.

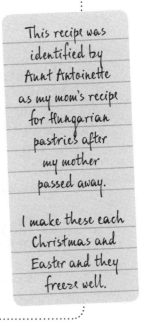

This recipe was identified by Aunt Antoinette as my mom's recipe for Hungarian pastries after my mother passed away.

I make these each Christmas and Easter and they freeze well.

This story comes from 1958, my teen years. Usually my boyfriend and I dated with another couple. The normal and expected thing to do was to go to church on Saturday and Sunday evenings and then return to the girl's house to play games, talk, and have refreshments. One Saturday when I was trying to decide what to make for refreshments that evening, my mom and dad said, "We are taking care of that this evening—just be sure to bring the other couple along home."

Were we ever surprised when we saw that my parents had bought and prepared lobster tails for us. I had never eaten lobster before. It was very expensive, just like it is now. Believe me it was some of the best food I ever ate. I could taste my parents' love in that lobster!   🍂 *Jeanette Oberholtzer*

🍂

Although my mother was primarily a dinner-oriented cook, she was also a supreme baker and breakfast maker. For our birthdays, she always made a special one-dish pancake for breakfast. It is similar to a Dutch baby pancake, I think. But for reasons unknown to all of us, it was always referred to as a David Eyre pancake.   🍂 *Kate Silverstein*

"David Eyre" Pancake
Kate Silverstein

½ cup flour
½ cup milk
2 eggs, beaten well
⅛ tsp. nutmeg
¼ cup butter
2 Tbsp. confectioners sugar
2 Tbsp. lemon juice

1. Preheat oven to 425°.
2. Combine flour, milk, eggs, and nutmeg in a medium bowl. Beat very well.
3. Melt butter in baking dish in oven. Pour in batter.
4. Return to oven and bake about 15 minutes. Sprinkle with sugar and lemon, and bake for 3 more minutes.

O ne year Mom worked at a restaurant that specialized in chicken. After closing up and supposedly throwing away the leftover chicken and veggies, she'd come home and make us chicken wraps with the works.

We'd have a choice between grilled or fried chicken with fresh lettuce, tomatoes, and beans. It tasted really good because Mom was the cook for the restaurant, and it was free.

When she had days off, which was very rare, we went back-roading—riding around a bunch of dirt roads and not really caring where we ended up. When we got to the middle of nowhere, we'd jump the fence and go for a walk. We got the money for gas by picking up cans along the roads.

On one of our back road hiking trips, we came across a rather large rattlesnake. After teaching us about the snake and how to react if we ever ran across another one, Mom killed it and took it home.

With great astonishment and mixed feelings, my sister and I helped Mom prepare the snake for dinner. We had deep-fried cornmeal-battered snake, mashed potatoes, and green beans. The best! 🖐 *Kathy*

M y birthday cake request each year was always the same: angel food cake with raspberry ice cream filling.

My mother always made my cake in her angel food cake pan that had a bakery name stamped on it. I am assuming that she bought a cake in the pan and paid a deposit to the bakery or perhaps got to keep the pan during a special offer. I still use that pan today—after too many birthdays to count!

And I did a variation on my favorite birthday cake for

my wedding. We had white cake with a raspberry filling. It was an attractive and very tasty cake, but it was not quite as good as my favorite birthday cakes. ❧ *Susan J. Heil*

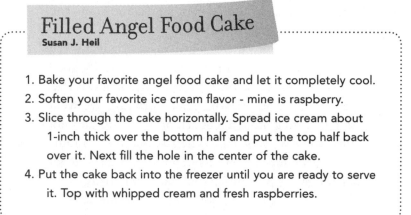

Filled Angel Food Cake
Susan J. Heil

1. Bake your favorite angel food cake and let it completely cool.
2. Soften your favorite ice cream flavor - mine is raspberry.
3. Slice through the cake horizontally. Spread ice cream about 1-inch thick over the bottom half and put the top half back over it. Next fill the hole in the center of the cake.
4. Put the cake back into the freezer until you are ready to serve it. Top with whipped cream and fresh raspberries.

❧

It was always a special treat to have popcorn in the evening. Since we raised our own, my brothers or dad would go to the barn where it was stored in a gunny sack.

I remember one time that they brought it in. When Mom opened it, out popped a mouse! That caused a lot of excitement as she really hated the little critters.

We'd rub the ears together to get the corn kernels off, take it outside, and blow off the chaff. Then Mom would pop it in the skillet with bacon grease. It probably wasn't very good for us, but it sure did taste good.

She'd pop a big dishpan full, and we'd eat until *we* popped. If there was any left over, we'd eat it for breakfast with milk and sugar. ❧ *Carolyn Spohn*

＊

When I was 5½ years old, my sister and I were placed in a foster home with the only real mom I have ever known, Mother M. We were very hungry, so she made us a batch of biscuits from scratch. We ate that whole batch with homemade jelly.

Mother M made another batch, and we ate every one of those, too! I will never forget Mother M and that day in my life. I still love homemade biscuits, sixty-three years later.

❧ *Marge Lange*

＊

Christmas time was always wonderful because we made cookies, lots of cookies. Sand tarts, snickerdoodles, Grandma's cutout sugar cookies, peanut butter cookies, and coconut snaps.

The sand tarts always got an egg wash, cinnamon, and a few chopped nuts. The sugar cookies got the red and green sprinkles. The duck, deer, gingerbread men, and the lady in the big skirt all got raisin eyes.

We always took the hot cookies to the shanty, an enclosed back porch for doing laundry, so they would cool quickly. The finished cookies were carefully packed in old lard or potato chip cans to keep them fresh. Sometimes we would have to have an extra baking evening, because the cookies disappeared too quickly. We wanted to have some left for Christmas dinner and Santa Claus.

I can still see Mother, in her red Christmas apron, hurrying out to the shanty with those coconut snaps. If she left them on the pan too long, they would stick. It she took them off too soon, they would crinkle up and not be pretty.

I loved coconut snaps best when they got stale. I liked them sticky and chewy—not fresh, crispy, and perfectly shaped. Imperfect things can be the best! That's just like some cooks I know—a little old and not so perfectly shaped.

❧ *Susan J. Heil*

Coconut Snaps
Susan J. Heil

1 quart molasses
2 pounds light brown sugar
¾ pound (3 sticks) butter
2 small fresh coconuts (Mother
    always used fresh coconut)
2½ pounds flour

We would drink the coconut milk as an extra treat.

1. Mix together. The batter is sort of thin.
2. Drop into cookies on baking sheet.
3. Bake at 325° for 6-8 minutes, until the bubbles are gone.

❧

There weren't many birthday traditions when I was growing up, but one thing my mom and I always did was bake and decorate my birthday cake together. I used to have a passion for horses, and Mom discovered an incredible, horse-head-shaped cake. I was thrilled, and it became a birthday tradition for several years.

I baked the cake, she cut it into the desired shape while I mixed the icing, and then we decorated it together. One year, we decided to try a different color of icing instead of the usual light yellow. We ended up with a rather unappetizing purple-grey, and used up all the powdered sugar in the process.

Once it was decorated, I tried to console myself that it didn't look terrible. But mostly I remember taking slices of that cake to school in my lunch and trying to hide them so nobody would notice or comment! 🍂 *Bethanny Baumer*

❦

When I was a child, my grandmothers lived 200 miles away. Even in the Depression years of the '30s, my parents and I made the trip "back home" to West Virginia at least once every three weeks. Grandma Snider always killed

Grandma Snider's Noodles
Jean Binns Smith

2 eggs
1 cup milk
1 tsp. salt
4 cups flour
2 tsp. baking powder

1. Beat egg and add to milk. Add dry ingredients and mix well. Mixture will be dry.
2. Place on a floured surface, roll thin and cut into strings about ⅓-inch wide.
3. Bring chicken broth to rolling boil in a kettle and drop noodles into it. Cook 15 minutes without taking off the lid.

This is Grandma Clara Rice Smith Snider's noodles recipe. I know of four generations that made noodles following this recipe. I have often wondered how many more generations were before the time my grandma handed it down to her daughter.

a chicken and made homemade noodles when we visited. To me, love is spelled N-O-O-D-L-E-S.

One of my earliest memories is sitting on the worn enamel counter of her old Hoosier cupboard turning the sifter in the flour bin as she rolled the dough and cut rows of noodles beside me using a kitchen knife. I am now 82. I think I was a good grandmother, babysitting grandchildren for working daughters, but never have I found the patience to let a child sit beside me, playing with a flour sifter while I made noodles.

> Sometimes a few of the noodles would stick together in a ball. Grandma always was upset and called these "sinkers." I thought they tasted best.

Homemade noodles were a favorite food of my father. I have often reflected about how fortunate he was. He had a mother-in-law, wife, daughter, daughter-in-law, and three granddaughters who enjoyed spoiling him by making homemade noodles.

I don't remember a lot about my mother when I was little. She was mentally ill and struggled with alcoholism. She was very pretty, and she took a lot of naps. I was to be quiet and take care of her. My mother liked to sew, and she made my dresses. I remember making doll clothes when she sewed.

  ❧ *Jean Binns Smith*

❧

We grew up in an era when children did not order a meal of special foods for their birthdays. Our birthday tradition was a freshly-baked angel food cake, usually without frosting. Dad raised cattle and pigs and had several small houses of laying hens, so we were never short on eggs.

Now to look at my mom, one might decide she is somewhat shy and reserved. Don't let that calm exterior fool you—

underneath is a mischievous spirit! She would try to lead us to conclude she hadn't had time to bake that day, which was completely believable with six children to raise, various hired men to feed in season, and a house and garden to oversee.

If we did see beaters or angel food pans in the sink, the cakes were for Mrs. Demmy, a customer who bought quantities of angel food cakes from Mom. As our evening meal progressed, Mom would vanish (to some secret location known only to mothers) only to reappear bearing a cake bright with the appropriate number of candles.

🌢 *Becky S. Frey*

🌿

Most people knew my mother as the doughnut lady, not because she was as round as a doughnut, but because she put her considerable energy into making and selling doughnuts. I have early memories of watching doughnuts sizzle in oil. These doughnuts were sold to our neighbors.

When I was 7 years old, the owner of the New Holland doughnut shop asked Mother if she would sell his day-old doughnuts. We started with Saturdays but soon were getting doughnuts every week day except Monday. We had plenty of customers. Everyone loved doughnuts, and Mother enjoyed all the people she met.

Doughnuts were only fifty cents a dozen. Our doughnut business ended in 1980 when we moved near the town of Intercourse. The hometown doughnut shop soon gave way to large grocery stores with their own bakeries.

🌢 *Brenda Hochstedler*

🌿

O ur birthdays were celebrated with a cake. One year, one of my aunts was at our house and made my birthday cake. I blew out the candles, and she cut the cake. My piece had a shiny silver quarter wrapped in wax paper between the layers. I was so excited. ✿ *Elsie Russett*

I would love to go back in time and help my mother make our rainbow pound cake. She would mix up the batter and divide the batter into several smaller bowls. It was always a challenge to find four or five bowls for this part of the process.

Pound Cake
Diane Blaising

1 cup (2 sticks) soft butter
1 cup sugar
¼ tsp. grated lemon zest
1 Tbsp. fresh lemon juice
4 large eggs
2 cups flour
¼ tsp. baking powder

1. Beat together butter and sugar. Beat in lemon zest and juice.
2. Beat in the eggs, one at a time, beating well after each one.
3. Beat in flour and baking powder.
4. Pour into greased and floured tube pan. Bake at 300° until a toothpick comes out clean when tested, about 75-90 minutes.

I would get to color each bowl of batter a different color. One got a few drops of blue, one green, one red, and one yellow. I could add two colors to the other bowls of batter to make orange and purple. The colored batter would be carefully spooned into a round tube cake pan, one colorful glob at a time.

Then the real magic happened. We took a knife and slowly ran it through the batter, pulling the colors ever so slightly into the neighboring colors. We could hardly wait until the cake was done and cool enough to slice. We were always amazed at the beautiful swirls of color. Beautiful, delicious slices of rainbow cake and cold milk with Mama in the kitchen—what could be more satisfying? ❧ *Diane Blaising*

One of the contributors to this book topped off her stories by saying, "Thanks for the opportunity to share some wonderful memories. Now I'm going to scoot and put some names and dates on my old and new photos, and also make sure somebody takes a couple shots of me!"

Let's all do it. And recall some good times with your mom, too.

Phyllis Pellman Good

Recipe Index

Dobash Cake, 102
Easy Baked Macaroni and Cheese, 147
Egg in a Hole, 11
Extra-Tender Pastry, 171
Filled Angel Food Cake, 198
French Dressing, 33
Fresh Harvard Beets, 81
Fudge, 60
Grandma Snider's Noodles, 201
Hamburger Stroganoff, 31
Hungarian Kiflis (Crescents), 194
Kolach, 150
Layer Cabbage, 129
Lemon Meringue Pie, 29
Lemon Rice, 116
Little Cheddar Loaves, 165
Macaroni Tuna Salad, 90
Major Grey Chicken, 98
Mama's Chocolate Pie, 189
Meatloaf, 49
Mock Apple Pie, 182
Mom's Magic Cherry Cobbler, 55
Mom's Rice and Chopmeat Stuffing, 167
Mush, 139
Nothing Cake, 101
Oatmeal Chocolate Chip Cookies, 66
Pineapple Torte, 45
Portuguese Sausage Soup, 136
Potato Salad, 90
Pound Cake, 204
Rivel Soup, 159
Salmon Croquettes, 157
Scalloped Salmon, 42
Tomato Pudding, 125
Tuna Noodle Casserole, 141

About the Authors

Phyllis Pellman Good is a *New York Times* bestselling author whose books have sold more than 12 million copies.

Good is the author of the nationally acclaimed *Fix-It and Forget-It* slow-cooker cookbooks, several of which have appeared on *The New York Times* bestseller list, as well as the bestseller lists of *USA Today*, *Publishers Weekly*, and *Book Sense*.

The series includes:

- *Fix-It and Forget-It Cookbook (Revised and Updated): 700 Great Slow-Cooker Recipes*
- *Fix-It and Forget-It Lightly (Revised and Updated): Healthy, Low-Fat Recipes for Your Slow Cooker*
- *Fix-It and Forget-It 5-Ingredient Favorites: Comforting Slow-Cooker Recipes*
- *Fix-It and Forget-It Christmas Cookbook: 600 Slow-Cooker Holiday Recipes*
- *Fix-It and Forget-It Diabetic Cookbook (Revised and Updated): 550 Slow Cooker Favorites—to Include Everyone* (with the American Diabetes Association)
- *Fix-It and Forget-It Vegetarian Cookbook: 565 Delicious Slow-Cooker, Stove-Top, Oven, and Salad Recipes, plus 50 Suggested Menus*
- *Fix-It and Forget-It PINK Cookbook: More Than 700 Great Slow-Cooker Recipes!*
- *Tips for Using Your Slow Cooker*

Good is also the author of the *Fix-It and Enjoy-It* series (featuring stove-top and oven recipes), a "cousin" series to the phenomenally successful *Fix-It and Forget-It* cookbooks.

Nearly all of the stories in this book have come from the friends of the *Fix-It and Forget-It* cookbooks—including our faithful recipe contributors from all over North America, followers of our Fix-It and Forget-It blog (fix-itandforget-it.com), and hundreds of thousands of our social media friends.

Join us on Facebook at www.facebook.com/fixitandforgetit
You can also find us on Twitter: @FixItForgetIt
Look for us on Pinterest: www.pinterest.com/FixitnForgetit